gettyimages

BON VOYAGE

An Oblique Glance at the World of Tourism

Ungewöhnliche Einblicke in die Welt des Tourismus

Regard inhabituel sur le monde du tourisme

teNeues

© 2002 teNeues Verlag GmbH + Co. KG
© 2002 Getty Images

⋆

Published worldwide by teNeues Publishing Group

teNeues Verlag/Book Division
Neuer Zollhof 1
40221 Düsseldorf
Germany
tel. +49 (0) 211-994597-0
fax +49 (0) 211-994597-40
email: books@teneues.de

teNeues Publishing Company
16 West 22nd Street
New York, N.Y. 10010
USA
tel. +1-212-627 9090
fax +1-212-627-9511

teNeues Publishing UK Ltd.
Aldwych House
71/91 Aldwych
London WC2B 4HN
UK
tel. +44-1892-837 171
fax +44-1892-837 272

teNeues France SARL
140, rue de la Croix Nivert
75015 Paris
France
tel. +33-1-55 76 62 05
fax +33-1-55 76 64 19

www.teneues.com

ISBN 3-8238-5577-8

Printed in Italy.

This book was produced by
Getty Images
21-31 Woodfield Road
London
W9 2BA
UK

While we strive for utmost precision in every detail, we cannot be held responsible
for any inaccuracies, nor for any subsequent loss or damage arising therefrom.

Die Deutsche Bibliothek — CIP-Einheitsaufnahme
Ein Titeldatensatz für diese Publikation ist bei der Deutschen Bibliothek erhältlich.

Design: Tea McAleer
Picture research: Ali Khoja
Text: Nick Yapp with Sarah Anderson
Translation: SWB Communications, Dr. Sabine Werner-Birkenbach,
Christine Cavrenne (french) and Elke Franz-Gaisser (german)
Idea and concept: Ralf Daab

OPPOSITE

Sun worshipping. The photographer
Inge Morath pays her homage
beneath azure skies over Acapulco,
January 1961.

OVERLEAF

Pussyfooting. Dee Hawks, wife of the
American film producer Howard
Hawks, sips her Jamaican cocktail of
fruit juices, 1958.

RECHTE SEITE

Sonnenanbeterin. Die Fotografin Inge
Morath hat sich unter dem blauen
Himmel von Acapulko ehrfürchtig der
Sonne zugewandt (Januar 1961).

FOLGENDE SEITE

Übervorsichtig. Dee Hawks, die Frau
des amerikanischen Filmproduzenten
Howard Hawks, nippt an ihrem ja-
maicanischen Fruchtcocktail (1958).

CI-CONTRE

Culte du soleil. La photographe
Inge Morath lui rend hommage sous
le ciel bleu d'Acapulco, janvier
1961.

AU VERSO

Attitude timorée. Dee Hawks, l'épouse
du producteur de films américain
Howard Hawks, sirote son cocktail de
jus de fruit jamaïcain, 1958.

gettyimages

Nick Yapp with Sarah Anderson

BON VOYAGE

An Oblique Glance at the World of Tourism
Ungewöhnliche Einblicke in die Welt des Tourismus
Regard inhabituel sur le monde du tourisme

teNeues

TRAVELLING
REISEN
VOYAGER

TWO COMMODITIES control the travel market – time and money. Travel consumes both in large quantities. It took a century and a half of struggle for shorter working hours and a decent level of pay to bring travel within the reach of the vast majority of people. And, even for the rich, the idea of travelling for enjoyment's sake is barely three hundred years old. Until roughly two hundred and fifty years ago, almost the only travellers – on land or sea – were soldiers, merchants and pilgrims – those ordered to travel, those paid to travel, and those bound by their faith to travel.

In the 18th century, a few wealthy people made the Grand Tour of Europe, seeking culture and a modicum of adventure. The Tour took roughly a year to complete and followed a well-worn itinerary – to Florence and Rome, Venice and Vienna, the village of Nice and the pleasure domes of Paris. Progress was slow, over roads and tracks that were ill-engineered and poorly maintained. Overnight stops were in draughty inns where the food was unappetising and the mattresses were bug-ridden. Danger was never far away – brigands, landslides, broken bridges, broken axles, broken bones.

One single invention changed all this – the steam locomotive. On Wednesday, 15th September 1830, the Duke of Wellington formally opened George Stephenson's *Liverpool and Manchester Railway* – the first entirely steam-hauled railway in the world. It was an immediate success. By 1850 there were over 3,600 miles

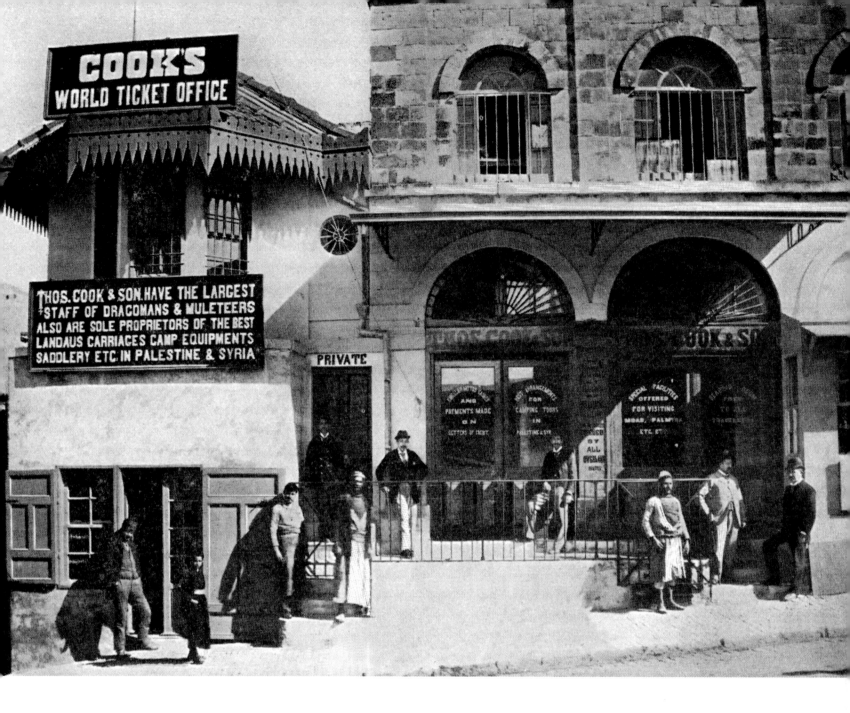

ABOVE

The *Thos Cook World Ticket Office*, Jerusalem at the beginning of the 20th century – the sign claims that 'THOS COOK & SON HAVE THE LARGEST STAFF OF DRAGOMANS & MULETEERS; ALSO ARE SOLE PROPRIETORS OF THE BEST LANDAUS, CARRIAGES, CAMP EQUIPMENTS, SADDLERY ETC. IN PALESTINE & SYRIA.

OPPOSITE

An Egyptian travel agent stands proudly beside his Ford de Luxe Roadster outside the Egyptian Travel Bureau in Luxor, 1940.

OBEN

Das *Thos Cook World Ticket Office* in Jerusalem zu Beginn des 20. Jahrhunderts – das Schild behauptet: "THOS COOK & SON VERFÜGT ÜBER DIE MEISTEN DRAGOMANE & MAULTIER-GESPANNE; AUSSERDEM SIND SIE BESITZER DER BESTEN LANDAUER, ZWEISPÄNNER, CAMPING-AUSRÜSTUNGEN, SATTELZEUGE ETC. IN PALÄSTINA & SYRIEN.

LINKE SEITE

Ein ägyptischer Reiseführer steht stolz neben seinem Ford de Luxe Roadster vor dem Ägyptischen Reisebüro in Luxor (1940).

EN-HAUT

Le guichet de l'agence *Thos Cook World*, Jérusalem au début du 20ème siècle – L'enseigne indique que « THOS COOK & FILS » A LE PERSONNEL LE PLUS NOMBREUX DE DROGMANS ET DE MULETIERS ; ELLE EST AUSSI LA SEULE PROPRIÉTAIRE DES MEILLEURS LANDAUS, ATTELAGES, MATÉRIEL DE CAMPEMENT, SELLERIE ETC. EN PALESTINE & EN SYRIE.

CI-CONTRE

Un agent de voyages égyptien pose fièrement près de sa roadster Ford de Luxe devant l'Agence de Voyages Égyptienne à Luxor, 1940.

ABOVE

Sleeping and dining cars on the *London Midland and Scottish Railway* are given their final polish at the company's Derby works, 23rd February 1937. It was the heyday of the long distance train, then the most comfortable and glamorous way to travel overland.

OPPOSITE

Conveyor belts load passengers' luggage on board a *White Star* liner at Tilbury Docks, London, August 1930.

OBEN

Schlaf- und Speisewagen der *London Midland and Scottish Railway* erhalten im Derby-Werk des Unternehmens den letzten Schliff (23. Februar 1937). Dies war die Blütezeit des Langstreckenzuges, der komfortabelsten und glanzvollsten Weise, über Land zu reisen.

RECHTE SEITE

Das Passagiergepäck gelangt über Förderbänder an Bord eines *White Star* Liniendampfers an den Tilbury Docks, London (August 1930).

EN-HAUT

Les wagons-restaurants et les wagons-lits de la compagnie *London Midland and Scottish Railway* finissent d'être astiqués au chantier de Derby de la compagnie, 23 février 1937. C'était l'âge d'or des trains à longue distance et, par la suite, la manière la plus confortable et la plus prestigieuse de voyager par voie de terre.

CI-CONTRE

Des tapis roulants transportent les bagages des voyageurs à bord d'un paquebot de ligne de la *White Star* à Tilbury Docks, Londres, août 1930.

of track in Britain alone. By 1870 there were railways operating in almost every country in the world – with over 50,000 miles of track in Western Europe, another 50,000 in North America, and over 11,000 miles in Tsarist Russia.

1870 was the *annus mirabilis* of rail travel. In that year it was possible to travel in considerable comfort on land and sea. The man responsible for bringing gracious living to the railway was George Mortimer Pullman, with his luxury coaches. The *New York Times* waxed lyrical on their splendour: 'Upon tables covered in snowy linen and garnished with services of solid silver, Ethiop waiters in spotless white placed a repast at which Delmonico himself could have had no occasion to blush.' Hot on Pullman's heels came Georges Nagelmackers. In 1872 he ran sleeping cars between Ostend and Berlin, Paris and Cologne, and Vienna and Munich. Six years later, he founded the *Compagnie Internationale des Wagon-Lits*, and in 1881 constructed the first custom-built restaurant car in Europe, with ceilings painted in Italian *stucco*, Spanish leather upholstery, and soap in the washrooms (a commodity still unknown in most hotels).

Every rail company competed to provide passengers with the greatest degree of luxury. On board the Trans-Siberian Express there was a library coach, and a Bechstein grand piano in the dining car. Dinner on the Wagon-Lits lasted three hours, and every coach had its complimentary bottle of Buchanan Scotch

BELOW

The horrors of sleeping where you have to. Passengers delayed by a go-slow of French air traffic controllers snatch a few moments of uncomfortable sleep in the passenger lounge at Heathrow Airport, London in June 1978.

OPPOSITE

Dressed in raincoats to face the delights of an English summer, passengers wait in relative comfort on benches in the concourse of Waterloo Station, London, August 1923. Waterloo was then the headquarters of the newly formed *Southern Railway*.

UNTEN

Der Schrecken, schlafen zu müssen, wo man gerade ist. Passagiere, Opfer eines französischen Fluglotsenstreiks, erhaschen im Warteraum des Flughafens Heathrow, London, ein paar Minuten unbequemen Schlafs (Juni 1978).

LINKE SEITE

In Regenmänteln gehüllt, um den Freuden des englischen Sommers zu trotzen, warten Passagiere in relativer Bequemlichkeit auf den Bänken der Bahnhofshalle von Waterloo Station, London (August 1923). Waterloo war seinerzeit das Hauptquartier der neu gegründeten *Southern Railway*.

EN BAS

L'horreur d'être contraint à dormir n'importe où. Les passagers retardés par une grève perlée des contrôleurs aériens français réussissent à trouver quelques moments de repos inconfortable dans la salle réservée aux passagers de l'aéroport d'Heathrow, Londres, juin 1978.

CI-CONTRE

Vêtus d'imperméables afin d'aborder les charmes d'un été anglais, les passagers attendent, assis sur des bancs au confort relatif, dans le hall de la gare de Waterloo, Londres, août 1923. Waterloo était alors le siège de la société *Southern Railway* nouvellement fondée.

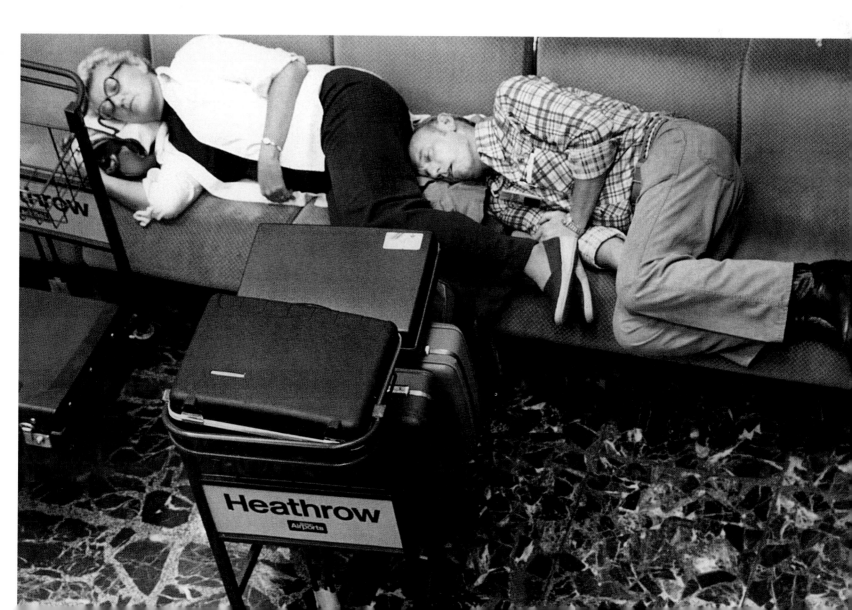

whisky and syphons of Schweppes soda water. Pullman's dining cars offered mountain-brook trout and bumpers of Krug champagne. The menu on chartered trains running between London and Liverpool for the Grand National in 1913 included plovers' eggs, roast quail, asparagus, and caviar on toast. Many crack trains served lobster and fillet steak as standard fare.

This golden age of rail travel lasted into the 1930s. 'Named' expresses roared across North America, South Africa and the length and breadth of Europe. There was the *Twentieth Century Limited* – New York to Chicago in streamlined elegance. There were the *Sunset Limited*, the *Broadway Limited*, the *Southern Crescent* and the Santa Fe *Super Chief*. And also in the United States there was the ultimate status symbol – the millionaire's private coach, tacked on to the train of its owners choice. Over in Europe 'bright young things' were whisked every day from Paris to the Cote d'Azur on *Le Train Bleu*, famous enough to inspire a ballet. Passengers on the *Flying Scotsman* enjoyed their breakfasts or their teas (the best of British meals) as they flashed through the countryside between London and Edinburgh. And, most glamorous of all, there was Georges Nagelmackers' *Orient Express*, with its reputation for romance and intrigue anywhere between the Gare de l'Est in Paris and Constantinople.

CLOCKWISE FROM BOTTOM LEFT

1980s affluence – Mrs Woolworth Donahue poses on her lavishly equipped motor yacht *Hartline*; 1940 pioneers – *Silver City Airways* disgorges its one car cargo at Le Touquet after its first cross Channel flight, 13th April 1949; 1920s style – a motoring party takes to the ferry plying between Venice and the Lido; 1960s crowds – a full load of cars, freight and passengers for the ferry between Naples and the islands of Capri and Ischia, August 1963.

VON LINKS UNTEN IM UHRZEIGERSINN

Wohlstand der Achtziger Jahre – Mrs. Woolworth Donahue posiert auf ihrer luxuriös ausgestatteten Motorjacht *Hartline*; Pioniere der vierziger Jahre – nach ihrem ersten Flug über den Kanal am 13. April 1949 entledigt sich die *Silver City Airways* in Le Toquet ihrer Fracht; Im Stil der zwanziger Jahre – eine Gesellschaft nimmt bei einem Autoausflug die zwischen Venedig und dem Lido verkehrende Fähre; Gedränge in den sechziger Jahren – eine komplette Ladung Autos, Fracht und Passagiere für die Fähre zwischen Neapel und den Inseln Capri und Ischia im August 1963.

DANS LE SENS DES AIGUILLES D'UNE MONTRE, A PARTIR DU BAS A GAUCHE

Les années quatre-vingts, années d'abondance – Mme Woolworth Donahue pose sur son yacht à moteur *Hartline*, somptueusement équipé. Les pionniers des années quarante – la *Silver City Airways* présente son avion-cargo pour une voiture au Touquet après sa première traversée de la Manche le 13 avril 1949. Le style des années vingt – un groupe d'automobilistes entre dans le ferry faisant la navette entre Venise et le Lido. Les foules des années soixante – un plein chargement de voitures, de marchandises et de passagers pour le ferry entre Naples et les îles de Capri et d'Ischia, août 1963.

Sailing ships on the *Collins Line* had smoking rooms, steam heating, ice to preserve food on the ten and a half day voyage across the Atlantic, and barbershops. But by 1870 real luxury arrived with the steamship – 'first class hotels that were made to float'. William Inman's *City of Rome* had a music room of ebony and gold. Samuel Cunard's *Aquitania* (reckoned by many the most beautiful of all transatlantic liners) was equipped with an Egyptian swimming-pool, a Carolingian smoking room, an Elizabethan grill, a Palladian lounge and suites that contained original paintings by Holbein, Velásquez, Van Dyck, Rembrandt, Reynolds and Gainsborough. The director of the *Hamburg-Amerika Line*, Albert Ballin, hired Escoffier to plan the kitchens on his liners and César Ritz to train his dining-room staff. The service on board such ships was impeccable, for the crew outnumbered the passengers.

Air travel has never been able to compete with style such as this, but, from the beginning, planes had the great advantage of speed. When the *Aircraft Travel and Transport Company* began the first scheduled fare-paying flights between London and Paris in 1919, the time for the journey was only two hours and twenty minutes, though passengers had to wear heavy coats (against the cold), and stuff their ears with cotton wool (for the engine noise was deafening). The following year *KLM* began regular services between Amsterdam and London, issuing their passengers with free postcard photographs of the pilots. By the late 1920s,

CLOCKWISE FROM OPPOSITE

The Fourth of July crowds at Nantasket Beach, Massachusetts, 1925; The ultimate in 1940s streamlined mobile homes; An inadequately camouflaged trailer breaks the skyline in Monument Valley, Arizona; Coins, stamps, helmets and bric-a-brac decorate a lorry used by disabled British ex-servicemen on their world tour, 1925.

LINKE SEITE BEGINNEND IM UHRZEIGERSINN

Menschenmenge am 4. Juli am Nantasket Beach, Massachusetts (1925); Das perfekte stromlinienförmige Wohnmobil der vierziger Jahre; Ein unzureichend getarnter Wohnwagen unterbricht die Silhouette des Monument Valley, Arizona; Münzen, Aufkleber, Helme und Nippes zieren einen Laster britischer Kriegsversehrter auf ihrer Weltreise (1925).

DANS LE SENS DES AIGUILLES D'UNE MONTRE, A PARTIR DE LA PHOTO CI-CONTRE

1925, les foules du quatre juillet sur la plage de Nantasket, Massachusetts. Le dernier des modèles des mobile homes aérodynamiques des années quarante. Une remorque camouflée de manière inadéquate rompt la ligne d'horizon dans la Monument Valley, Arizona. Des pièces, des timbres, des casques et du bric-à-brac décorent un camion utilisé par des anciens soldats britanniques handicapés, lors de leur tournée dans le monde en 1925.

Just a few hundred metres from the Wall Street crash, a *Dornier DO X* flying boat floats safely berthed in New York Harbour, 1929. Flying boats had an excellent safety record during their comparatively short commercial lifetime, and had the added of advantage in the case of many destinations, of being able to land far nearer the city centre than conventional airliners.

Nur wenige hundert Meter von der Wall Street landet ein *Dornier DO X* Wasserflugzeug sicher im New Yorker Hafen (1929). Während ihrer vergleichsweise kurzen Zeit der kommerziellen Nutzung hatten die Wasserflugzeuge in Bezug auf ihre Sicherheit einen guten Ruf und erfreuten sich zusätzlicher Vorteile, da sie wesentlich näher an den Stadtzentren landen konnten als konventionelle Flugzeuge.

À quelques centaines de mètres seulement de l'endroit du crash de Wall Street, un hydravion *Dornier DO X* amarré au port de New York flotte paisiblement en 1929. Au cours de leur relativement brève exploitation commerciale, les hydravions offraient un excellent standard de sécurité et l'avantage supplémentaire, en cas de nombreuses destinations, de pouvoir amerrir beaucoup plus près du centre-ville que des avions conventionnels.

Imperial Airways were flying in series of hops to the Near East, Africa, India and even as far as Australia. Meals were served on board. *Lufthansa* planes had reclining seats. There were even in-flight silent movies.

On transatlantic flights, the giant airships were quieter, steadier in flight and far more comfortable. Passengers on the *Hindenburg* sipped their LZ 129 Frosted Cocktails (gin with a dash of orange juice) before settling down to 'Fattened duckling Bavarian style with champagne cabbage' or 'Venison cutlets Beauval with Berny potatoes' as they drifted smoothly over the ocean. 'The *Graf Zeppelin*,' reported Lady Grace Drummond Hay, 'is more than just machinery, canvas and aluminium. It has a soul.' But the soul of the airship was destroyed on 6th May 1937, when the *Hindenburg* burst into flames as it struggled to reach the mooring mast at Lakehurst, New Jersey. Just fourteen years later, the De Havilland *Comet*, the world's first jet passenger airliner, took to the skies. By the late 1950s, air travel had become the fastest and the cheapest means of inter-continental travel, and threatened to put an end to its rivals.

But it didn't. The excitement of travel remains in all its forms – road, rail, ship and plane. The *Orient Express* was reborn in the 1980s. There are as many cruise ships sailing the seas today as there were fifty years ago. Every year the skies become more crowded with sleek airliners carrying pleasure seekers to all parts of the world. And still there are those magic moments when the last piece of luggage is stowed in the car, or when the backpack is hoisted on to the shoulders…and the journey begins.

ZWEI GÜTER beherrschen den Reisemarkt – Zeit und Geld. Reisen verzehrt beides in großen Mengen. Eineinhalb Jahrhunderte des Kampfes waren notwendig, um durch kürzere Arbeitszeiten und ein passables Lohnniveau der überwältigenden Mehrheit der Menschen das Reisen zu ermöglichen. Zudem ist die Idee des Reisens aus purem Vergnügen, selbst für die Reichen, kaum dreihundert Jahre alt. Bis vor rund zweihundertfünfzig Jahren bestand die Mehrheit der Reisenden – über Land oder auf dem Wasser – aus Soldaten, Händlern und Pilgern, also denen, denen man zu reisen befohlen hatte, denen, die für das Reisen bezahlt wurden, und denen, die sich durch ihren Glauben zum Reisen verpflichtet fühlten.

   Während des 18. Jahrhunderts begaben sich einige wenige wohlhabende Menschen auf die *Grand Tour* durch Europa, auf der Suche nach Kultur und einem Quäntchen Abenteuer. Diese dauerte rund ein Jahr und folgte einer bewährten Reiseroute: Florenz, Rom, Venedig, Wien, Nizza und zu den Pariser Vergnügungstempeln. Man kam nur langsam vorwärts, über schlecht angelegte und gewartete Straßen und Wege. Man übernachtete in zugigen Gasthäusern mit unappetitlichem Essen und Ungeziefer verseuchten Matratzen. Gefahren warteten hinter jeder Ecke – Räuber, Erdrutsche, eingestürzte Brücken, gebrochene Achsen oder Knochen.

OPPOSITE

OPPOSITE

The Ford Transit motor-caravan interior is almost timeless, but the crocheted waistcoat and flared jeans reveal that this must be the 1970s. And the empty driver's seat suggests that 'Dad' took this publicity picture.

BELOW

A woman camper cooks her solitary supper as dusk falls over the wilds of Utah, USA.

LINKE SEITE

Die Innenausstattung des Ford Transit-Wohnmobils ist nahezu zeitlos, doch Häkelweste und Jeans mit Schlag zeigen, dass dies die siebziger Jahre sind. Der leere Fahrersitz lässt darauf schließen, dass „Papa" dieses Werbe-foto geschossen hat.

UNTEN

Eine Camperin bereitet ihr einsames Abendessen zu, während die Dämmerung über die Wildnis Utahs, USA, hereinbricht.

CI-CONTRE

L'intérieur du camping-car Ford Transit est presque intemporel, mais le gilet crocheté et les jeans évasés indiquent qu'il doit s'agir des années soixante-dix. Le siège vide du conducteur laisse suggérer que c'est « papa » qui prend cette photo de publicité.

EN BAS

Une campeuse prépare son dîner en solitaire alors que le soleil se couche sur les vastes étendues de l'Utah, USA.

Cocktails for the pilots, 'smoking permitted' and everyone with a window seat. Inside an *Air Dispatch Croydon-to-Paris luxury Air Speed Envoy* (1936).

Cocktails für die Piloten, „Rauchen gestattet" und einen Fensterplatz für jeden: In einem luxuriösen *Air Dispatch Croydon-Paris Air Speed Envoy* (1936).

Des cocktails pour les pilotes, permission de fumer et un siège à la fenêtre pour tout le monde. À l'intérieur d'un avion de luxe *Air Dispatch Air Speed Envoy Croydon-Paris* (1936).

Eine einzige Erfindung veränderte all dies – die Dampflokomotive. Am Mittwoch, dem 15. September 1830 weihte der Duke of Wellington feierlich Stephenson's *Liverpool and Manchester Railway* ein – die erste vollständig dampfbetriebene Eisenbahn der Welt. Sie wurde auf Anhieb ein Erfolg. Im Jahre 1850 gab es alleine in Großbritannien bereits ein Schienennetz von über 5.800 km Länge. Im Jahre 1870 existierten in fast jedem Land der Welt Eisenbahngesellschaften. Die Länge der Schienennetze betrug über 80.000 km in Westeuropa, weitere 80.000 km in Nordamerika und 17.600 km im zaristischen Russland.

1870 war das *annus mirabilis* der Zugreise. In diesem Jahr wurde das Reisen mit einem beträchtlich gesteigerten Komfort zu Lande und zu Wasser möglich. Der Mann, der die Eisenbahn mit luxuriösen Waggons zu kultiviertem Leben erweckte, war George Mortimer Pullman. Die *New York Times* geriet über ihre Pracht ins Schwärmen: „Auf Tischen, gedeckt mit schneeweißem Leinen und einem Service aus massivem Silber, richten in ebenso makelloses Weiß gekleidete äthiopische Kellner ein Mahl an, dessen sich auch Delmonico höchstpersönlich nicht zu schämen bräuchte." Pullman hart auf den Fersen war Georges Nagelmackers. 1872 betrieb er Schlafwagen zwischen Ostende und Berlin, Paris und Köln sowie Wien und München. Sechs Jahre später gründete er die *Compagnie Internationale des Wagon-Lits*. 1881 konstruierte er den ersten speziell angefertigten Speisewagen Europas mit Deckengemälden im Stile des italienischen *Stucco*, mit spanischem Leder bezogenen Polstersitzen und Seife in den Waschräumen (einer selbst in den meisten Hotels noch unbekannten Errungenschaft).

Alle Eisenbahngesellschaften konkurrierten darum, ihren Passagieren den größtmöglichen Luxus zu bieten. An Bord der Transsibirischen Eisenbahn befanden sich ein Bibliotheks-Waggon sowie ein Bechsteinflügel im Speisewagen. Das Dinner bei *Wagon-Lits* dauerte drei Stunden und in jedem Abteil standen kostenlos eine Flasche *Buchanan Scotch Whisky* und gekühltes Schweppes Soda zur Verfügung. In Pullmans Speisewagen wurden Bergbachforellen und Spezialabfüllungen von Krug-Champagner serviert. Das Menü in Charterzügen zwischen London und Liverpool der *Grand National* bestand 1913 unter anderem aus Kiebitzeiern, gebratenen Wachteln, Spargel und Kaviartoast. Zahlreiche Luxuszüge servierten Hummer und Filetsteaks als Standardkost.

Dieses goldene Zeitalter der Zugreisen dauerte bis in die Dreißiger Jahre des 20. Jahrhunderts an. „Namhafte" Expresszüge brausten durch Nordamerika, Südafrika und kreuz und quer durch Europa. Es gab den *Twentieth Century Limited* – in stromlinienförmiger Eleganz von New York nach Chicago. Es gab den *Sunset Limited*, den *Broadway Limited*, den *Southern Crescent* sowie den *Santa Fe Super Chief*. Zudem gab es in den Vereinigten Staaten das ultimative Statussymbol – die Privatwaggons der Millionäre, angehängt an einen Zug nach Wahl des Besitzers. Drüben in Europa sausten mit *Le Train Bleu* jeden Tag „hübsche, junge Dinger" von Paris an die Cote d'Azur, was ihn berühmt genug machte, um zu einem Ballet zu inspirieren. Passagiere des *Flying Scotsman* genossen ihr Frühstück oder ihren Tee (die Beste der englischen Mahlzeiten), während sie die Landschaft zwischen London und Edinburgh durchquerten. Der Glanzvollste von allen war jedoch Georges Nagelmackers *Orient Express*, berüchtigt für Romanzen und Intrigen an Bord auf dem Weg zwischen dem Gare de l'Est in Paris und Konstantinopel.

Die Segelschiffe der *Collins Line* verfügten über Rauchersalons, Dampfheizung, Eis, um die Lebensmittel auf der zehneinhalb Tage dauernden Reise über den Atlantik frisch zu halten, sowie Friseurläden. Der wahre

Luxus kam jedoch 1870 mit den Dampfschiffen – den „schwimmenden First-Class-Hotels". William Inmans *City of Rome* besaß einen in Ebenholz und Gold gehaltenen Musiksalon. Samuel Cunards *Aquitania* (für viele der damals schönste Atlantikliner) war mit einem ägyptischen Swimmingpool, einem karolingischen Rauchsalon, einem elisabethanischen Grillroom, einem palladianischen Salon sowie Suiten mit Originalgemälden von Holbein, Velázquez, van Dyck, Rembrandt, Reynolds und Gainsborough ausgestattet. Der Direktor der *Hamburg-Amerika-Line*, Albert Ballin, ließ Escoffier die Küchen auf seinen Passagierschiffen entwerfen und César Ritz die Bedienungen für die Restaurants ausbilden. Der Service an Bord dieser Schiffe war tadellos, denn die Anzahl der Crewmitglieder überstieg die Anzahl der Passagiere.

Flugreisen konnten mit solch einem Stil nie konkurrieren, doch hatten die Flugzeuge von Anfang an den großen Vorteil der Geschwindigkeit. Als die *Aircraft Travel and Transport Company* im Jahre 1919 ihre ersten regulären Flüge zwischen London und Paris aufnahm, dauerte die Reise nur zwei Stunden und zwanzig Minuten, auch wenn die Reisenden dabei dicke Mäntel (gegen die Kälte) tragen und ihre Ohren mit Baumwollstöpseln verschließen mussten (der Lärm der Maschinen war ohrenbetäubend). Im darauf folgenden Jahr nahm *KLM* den Linienverkehr zwischen Amsterdam und London auf und verteilte kostenlose Postkartenbilder der Piloten an die Passagiere. Ende der zwanziger Jahre flog *Imperial Airways* mit vielen

ABOVE

Trans-continental passengers are roused from their slumbers in a railway siding near Lake Windemere, British Columbia, Canada, 24th July 1927. As well as kitchen and dining saloons, the train was equipped with sleeping cars, but the heat was so intense that many preferred to sleep in the open.

OPPOSITE

The New York-Albany railroad advertising poster.

OBEN

Transkontinental-Reisende werden auf einem Abstellgleis nahe Lake Windemere, Britisch Kolumbien, Kanada, aus ihrem Schlummer geweckt (24. Juli 1927). Neben Küche und Speisewagen war der Zug außerdem mit Schlafwagen ausgestattet. Die Hitze war jedoch so groß, dass viele es vorzogen, im Freien zu schlafen.

LINKE SEITE

Das Werbeplakat für die Zuglinie New York-Albany.

EN-HAUT

Les passagers transcontinentaux sont tirés de leur sommeil sur une voie de garage près du lac Windemere, Colombie britannique, Canada, 24 juillet 1927. Outre la cuisine et les salles de restaurant, le train comprenait des wagons-lits, mais la chaleur était tellement intense que beaucoup préféraient dormir en plein air.

CI-CONTRE

Affiche publicitaire des chemins de fer New-York-Albany.

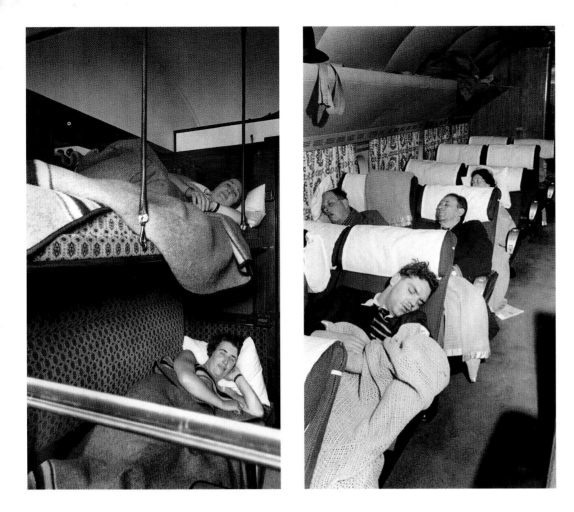

CLOCKWISE FROM LEFT

Third class sleeping accommodation on the *London Midland and Scottish Railway* in the late 1920; The pattern of sleep for the future – travellers crash out on an American airliner, December 1951; Author, columnist and *bon vivant* Lucius Beebe enjoys champagne and a fine cigar in his personal railroad car *Virginia City*, 1960. Note the solid marble gas-fuelled log fire.

VON LINKS IM UHRZEIGERSINN

Schlafen dritter Klasse bei der *London Midland and Scottish Railway* (Ende der zwanziger Jahre); Der Schlaf der Zukunft – Reisende schlummern an Bord eines amerikanischen Linienflugzeuges (Dezember 1951); Autor, Kolumnist und Bonvivant Lucius Beebe genießt in seinem privaten Eisenbahnwaggon *Virginia City* Champagner und eine feine Zigarre (1960). Man beachte den gasgefeuerten Kamin aus solidem Marmor.

DANS LE SENS DES AIGUILLES D'UNE MONTRE, A PARTIR DE LA GAUCHE

Couchettes de la troisième classe de la *London Midland and Scottish Railway* à la fin des années vingt. La façon de dormir du futur – les voyageurs tombent de sommeil sur un avion de ligne américain, décembre 1951. Lucius Beebe, auteur, éditorialiste et bon vivant savoure un excellent cigare et du champagne dans son wagon personnel *Virginia City*, 1960. À noter: la cheminée en marbre massif du feu ouvert fonctionnant au gaz.

Zwischenstops in den Nahen Osten, nach Afrika, Indien und sogar ins ferne Australien. An Bord wurden Mahlzeiten gereicht. *Lufthansa*-Flugzeuge verfügten über Liegesitze. Selbst Stummfilme gab es während des Fluges zu sehen.

Die riesigen Luftschiffe der Transatlantik-Linien waren leiser, flogen ruhiger und boten weit mehr Komfort. Die Passagiere der *Hindenburg* schlürften ihre *LZ 129 Frosted Cocktails* (Gin mit einem Spritzer Orangensaft) bevor sie sich zu bayerischer Mastente mit Champagnerkraut oder Rehmedaillons *Beauval* mit Berner Kartoffeln niederließen und dabei sanft über den Ozean hinweg glitten. „Das Luftschiff *Graf Zeppelin*", so berichtete Lady Grace Drummond Hay, „ist mehr als nur eine Maschinerie, bestehend aus Leinwand und Aluminium. Es hat eine Seele." Doch die Seele der Luftschiffe wurde am 6. Mai 1937 zerstört, als die *Hindenburg* bei dem Versuch, den Ankermast in Lakehurst, New Jersey, zu erreichen, in Flammen aufging. Nur vierzehn Jahre später stieg der erste Passagier-Düsenjet der Welt, der *Comet* von De Havilland, in den Himmel. Ende der fünfziger Jahre war die Flugreise zur schnellsten und billigsten Möglichkeit für Interkontinentalreisen geworden und drohte, ihren Rivalen ein Ende zu bereiten.

Doch dies geschah nicht. Das Aufregende am Reisen blieb in all seinen Formen erhalten – auf der Straße, mit Zug, Schiff und Flugzeug. In den Achtziger Jahren feierte der *Orient Express* seine Wiedergeburt. Heute gibt es ebenso viele Kreuzfahrtschiffe auf den Meeren wie vor fünfzig Jahren. Jedes Jahr tummeln sich mehr stromlinienförmige Verkehrsflugzeuge am Himmel, die Vergnügungssuchende in alle Teile der Welt bringen. Und immer noch sind da diese magischen Momente, wenn das letzte Gepäckstück im Auto verstaut oder der Rucksack geschultert ist... und die Reise beginnt.

DEUX MATIERÈS PREMIÈRES contrôlent le marché des voyages – le temps et l'argent. Les voyages consomment les deux en grande quantité. Un siècle et demi de lutte pour une réduction du temps de travail et un niveau décent de rémunération a été nécessaire pour que voyager soit à la portée de la large majorité des citoyens. De plus, même pour les riches, l'idée de voyager à des seules fins de divertissement ne date que de trois cents ans à peine. Jusqu'à environ deux cent cinquante ans, les seuls voyageurs – sur terre et sur mer – étaient des soldats, des marchands et des pèlerins – ceux qui recevaient l'ordre, étaient payés ou étaient guidés par leur foi pour voyager.

Au 18ème siècle, quelques nantis entreprirent le grand tour d'Europe à la recherche de culture et d'un minimum d'aventure. Il fallait environ un an pour suivre un itinéraire préétabli – à Florence et à Rome, à Venise et à Vienne, au village de Nice et aux palais du plaisir de Paris. La progression était lente sur des routes et des sentiers mal construits et mal entretenus. La nuit, les voyageurs s'arrêtaient dans des auberges pleines de courants d'air où la nourriture était peu appétissante et les matelas étaient infestés de punaises. Le danger n'était jamais loin – que ce soient les brigands, les éboulements, les ponts cassés, les essieux cassés ou les os cassés.

Il a suffi d'une seule invention pour changer tout cela – la locomotive à vapeur. Mercredi 15 septembre 1830, le Duc de Wellington inaugura la ligne de chemin de fer de George Stephenson allant de Liverpool à Manchester – la première ligne fonctionnant entièrement à la vapeur dans le monde. Ce fut un succès immédiat. En 1850, la Grande-Bretagne comptait à elle seule plus de 5.800 km de lignes de chemin de fer. En 1870, des trains circulaient dans presque tous les pays du monde avec plus de 80.000 km de lignes en Europe de l'Ouest, environ 80.000 km en Amérique du Nord et plus de 17.600 km dans la Russie du tsar.

1870 fut l'*annus mirabilis* des voyages par chemins de fer. Cette année-là, il était possible de voyager très confortablement par mer et par terre. C'est George Mortimer Pullman qui a été responsable de l'amélioration du confort et du raffinement dans les trains grâce à ses wagons de luxe. Le *New York Times* s'enthousiasmait sur leurs splendeurs en ces termes : « Des serveurs éthiopiens vêtus de blanc immaculé apportent sur des tables drapées de nappes blanches soyeuses et garnies de services en argent des mets qui n'auraient pas pu faire rougir Delmonico lui-même. » Directement après Pullman, arriva Georges Nagelmackers. En 1872, ses wagons-lits circulaient entre Ostende et Berlin, Paris et Cologne et Vienne et Munich. Six ans plus tard, il fonda la *Compagnie Internationale des Wagons-lits* et construisit en 1881 le premier wagon-restaurant conçu pour ses clients en Europe avec des plafonds ornés de stuc italien, des banquettes en cuir d'Espagne et du savon dans les toilettes (un détail encore inconnu dans la plupart des hôtels).

Chaque compagnie de chemins de fer rivalisait pour offrir à ses passagers le plus de luxe possible. À bord du Trans-Sibérien express, on trouvait un wagon-bibliothèque et un grand piano Bechstein dans le wagon-restaurant. Le dîner sur les Wagons-lits durait trois heures et chaque wagon avait sa bouteille de whisky Buchanan gratuite et des siphons de Schweppes à disposition. Les wagons-restaurants Pullman offraient des truites de ruisseaux de montagne et des rasades de champagne Krug. Le menu sur les trains charter

CLOCKWISE FROM ABOVE

The swimming pool on board the
SS Coama in the early 1930s; An *Orient
Line* poster; *Grace Line* – out of New
York and heading south,1935; Mixed
doubles on the *SS Cap Areona*, 1928.

OBEN BEGINNEND IM
UHRZEIGERSINN

Der Swimmingpool an Bord der
SS Coama Anfang der 1930er-Jahre;
Ein Plakat der *Orient Line; Grace
Line* – von New York nach Süden
(1934); Gemischtes Doppel auf der
SS Cap Areona (1928).

DANS LE SENS DES AIGUILLES D'UNE
MONTRE, A PARTIR DU HAUT

La piscine à bord du *SS Coama* au
début des années trente. Un poster de
l' *Orient Line. Grace Line* – au départ
de New York et en direction du sud,
1935. Double mixte sur le *SS Cap
Areona*, 1928.

ORIENT LINE TO AUSTRALIA, PACIFIC, NORTH AMERICA AND FAR EAST

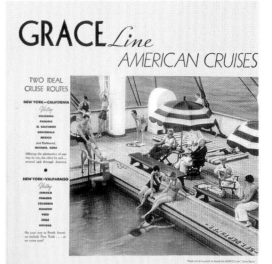

ABOVE

Patsy Pulitzer checks the contents of her bag before switching from car to a monoplane belonging to the *Everglades Flying Service* at Palm Beach, Florida in 1955.

OPPOSITE

Surrounded by private speedboats, a private helicopter, maps, brochures, ice buckets and all the panoply of luxury, Roy J Craven and Prince Pouilnac pass a pleasant afternoon in Monte Carlo harbour, August 1976. Two archetypal Slim Aarons photographs.

OBEN

Patsy Pulitzer prüft den Inhalt ihrer Tasche, bevor sie vom Auto in einen Eindecker des *Everglades Flying Service* in Palm Beach, Florida, umsteigt (1955).

RECHTE SEITE

Umgeben von privaten Schnellbooten, einem Privathubschrauber, Karten, Prospekten, Eiskübeln und der ganzen Palette des Luxus, verbringen Roy J. Craven und Prinz Pouilnac einen angenehmen Nachmittag im Hafen von Monte Carlo (August 1976). Zwei typische Slim-Aarons-Fotografien.

EN-HAUT

Patsy Pulitzer vérifie le contenu de son sac avant de passer de sa voiture dans un avion monoplace appartenant à *Everglades Flying Service* à Palm Beach, Floride en 1955.

CI-CONTRE

Entourés de hors-bord privés, d'un hélicoptère privé, de cartes, de brochures, de seaux à glace et de toute la panoplie de luxe, Roy J Craven et le Prince Pouilnac passent un agréable après-midi au port de Monte Carlo, août 1976. Deux photographies archétypes de Slim Aarons.

circulant entre Londres et Liverpool pour le Grand National de 1913 comprenait des œufs de pluviers, des cailles rôties, des asperges et des toasts au caviar. De nombreux trains parmi les plus fameux servaient du homard et des filets de bœuf comme nourriture standard.

L'âge d'or du transport par chemins de fer dura jusque dans les années trente. Toutes sortes d'express vrombissaient à travers l'Amérique du Nord, l'Afrique du Sud et parcouraient l'Europe en long et en large. Le *Twentieth Century Limited* New York – Chicago par exemple dans toute son élégance aérodynamique. Il y avait le *Sunset Limited*, le *Broadway Limited*, le *Southern Crescent* et le *Super Chief* de Santa Fe. Aux États-Unis, on trouvait même le dernier symbole de statut – le wagon privé du millionnaire qui pouvait être attaché au train de son choix. Outre-Atlantique, en Europe, les jeunes gens brillants étaient entraînés chaque jour de Paris jusqu'à la Côte d'Azur sur le *Train Bleu*, assez fameux pour inspirer un ballet. Les passagers du *Flying Scotsman* savouraient leur petit-déjeuner ou leur thé (le meilleur des repas anglais) tout en traversant la campagne entre Londres et Édimbourg. Enfin, le plus prestigieux de tous, l'*Orient Express* de Georges Nagelmackers réputé pour ses intrigues et ses romances partout entre la Gare de l'Est de Paris et Constantinople.

OPPOSITE

Victorian tourists gather on the summit of Mount Vesuvius, Italy, 1888. Twenty years earlier, the American writer Mark Twain described the scene at the top: '…brilliant with yellow banks of sulphur and with lava and pumice-stone of many colours. No fire was visible anywhere, but gusts of sulphurous steam issued from a thousand little cracks and fissures…'

BELOW

Exhausted pedicab drivers await new customers on a street in Java, Indonesia.

LINKE SEITE

Viktorianische Touristen auf dem Gipfel des Vesuv, Italien (1888). Zwanzig Jahre früher beschrieb der amerikanische Schriftsteller Mark Twain die Gipfelszene so: „…strahlend, mit gelben Schwefelbänken sowie vielfarbiger Lava und Bimssteinformationen. Nirgendwo war Feuer sichtbar, doch schwefelige Dampfwolken strömten aus Tausenden kleiner Spalten und Risse…"

UNTEN

Erschöpfte Rikscha-Fahrer warten an einer Straße auf Java, Indonesien, auf neue Kundschaft.

CI-CONTRE

Des touristes de l'ère victorienne se rassemblent au sommet du Vésuve, Italie, 1888. Vingt ans plus tôt, l'écrivain Mark Twain décrivait la scène au sommet comme suit : « …brillant de par ses bancs jaunes de souffre, sa lave et sa pierre ponce de toutes les couleurs. Le feu n'était visible à aucun endroit, mais des bouffées de vapeurs sulfureuses s'échappaient de milliers de petites fentes et de fissures… »

EN BAS

Des conducteurs de cyclo-pousse exténués attendent des nouveaux clients dans une rue de Java, Indonésie.

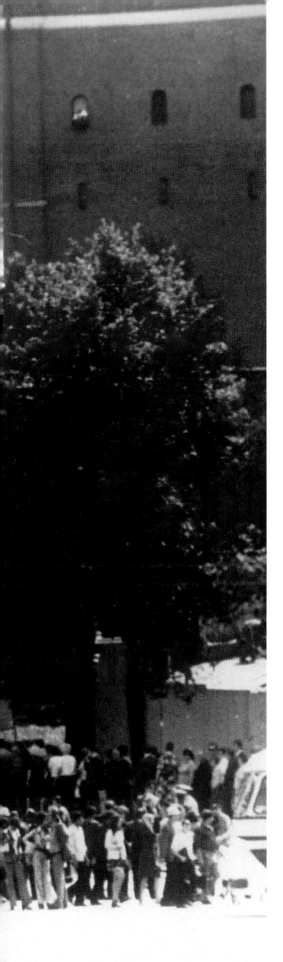

CLOCKWISE FROM LEFT

An *Intourist* coach pulls up in Red Square, Moscow and its passengers join the daily queue that winds up to the Kremlin. The visitors are all waiting to see the tomb of Lenin; '…and here we are in sunny Stresa…or Venice…or Sorrento, Capri, Rome, Florence…' Tour guide Margaret Newton of *British Cars* keeps her party informed and up to date on a coach trip through Italy, June 1954; An early attempt at *dètente*. An *American Express* travel poster of 1934 advertises the joys of 'New Russia'.

VON LINKS IM UHRZEIGERSINN

Ein *Intourist*-Bus hält am Roten Platz in Moskau und die Passagiere reihen sich in die tägliche Schlange vor dem Kreml ein. Die Besucher wollen das Mausoleum Lenins sehen; „…und hier befinden wir uns im sonnigen Stresa… oder Venedig… oder Sorrent, Capri, Rom, Florenz…" Reiseleiterin Margret Newton von *British Cars* hält ihre Reisegruppe während einer Busreise durch Italien auf dem Laufenden (Juni 1954); Ein früher Versuch der Entspannungspolitik: Ein Reiseplakat von *American Express* 1934 wirbt für die Freuden des „Neuen Russland".

DANS LE SENS DES AIGUILLES D'UNE MONTRE, A PARTIR DE LA GAUCHE

Un car de la societé *Intourist* s'arrête sur la Place Rouge de Moscou et ses passagers se joignent à la file quotidienne qui chemine vers le Kremlin. Les visiteurs attendent tous de voir la tombe de Lénine. « … Et nous voici maintenant dans la ville ensoleillée de Stresa…ou à Venise…ou à Sorrente, Capri, Rome, Florence… » la guide touristique Margaret Newton de la société *British Cars* donne des informations à son public lors d'une excursion en car à travers l'Italie, juin 1954. Un premier signe de la détente. Un poster de voyages de l'*American Express* de 1934 vante les joies de la « Nouvelle Russie ».

A plane load of enthusiastic tourists arrives in Almeria, southern Spain in the 1950s. The leader clearly can't wait to be first in the swimming pool.

Ein Flugzeug voller begeisterter Urlauber bei der Ankunft in Almeria, Südspanien (in den Fünfziger Jahren). Der Gruppenleiter kann es offensichtlich nicht erwarten, als erster den Swimmingpool zu stürmen.

Un avion rempli de touristes enthousiastes arrive à Alméria, au sud de l'Espagne dans les années cinquante. Le responsable est manifestement impatient d'être le premier à plonger dans la piscine.

Les bateaux à voile de la *Collins Line* avaient des fumoirs, le chauffage à vapeur, de la glace pour préserver la nourriture pendant une traversée de l'Atlantique de dix jours et demi et des salons de coiffure. Toutefois, c'est en 1870 qu'arriva le vrai luxe, avec les bateaux à vapeur – « des hôtels de 1ère classe conçus pour flotter ». Le *City of Rome* de William Inman avait une salle de musique en or et en ébène. *L'Aquitania* de Samuel Cunard (considéré par beaucoup comme le plus beau paquebot de grande ligne transatlantique) était équipé d'une piscine égyptienne, d'un fumoir carolingien, d'un grill élisabethain, d'un salon conçu dans le style de l'architecte Palladio et de suites qui contenaient des peintures originales de Holbein, Vélasquez, Van Dijk, Rembrandt, Reynolds et Gainsborough. Le directeur de la *Hamburg-Amerika Line*, Albert Ballin, engagea Escoffier pour planifier les cuisines de ses paquebots et César Ritz pour former le personnel de salle. Le service à bord de tels bateaux était impeccable puisque les membres du personnel étaient plus nombreux que les passagers.

Le transport aérien n'a jamais pu rivaliser en style avec ces moyens de transport, mais, dès le début, les avions ont offert le grand avantage de la vitesse. Lorsque la Aircraft Travel and Transport Company lança en 1919 ses premiers vols réguliers à tarifs entre Londres et Paris, le voyage ne durait que deux heures et vingt minutes. Cependant les voyageurs devaient porter des manteaux épais (contre le froid) et devaient se boucher les oreilles avec du coton (le bruit des moteurs étant assourdissant). L'année suivante, la *KLM* commença des services réguliers entre Amsterdam et Londres offrant à ses passagers des cartes postales gratuites avec des photos des pilotes. À la fin des années 1920, l'Imperial Airways volait en plusieurs étapes jusqu'au Proche-Orient, en Afrique, en Inde et même aussi loin qu'en Australie. Des repas étaient servis à bord. Les avions de la Lufthansa avaient des sièges inclinables. Des films muets pouvaient même être visionnés en vol.

Pour les vols transatlantiques, les dirigeables étaient plus silencieux, plus stables en vol et beaucoup plus confortables. Les passagers de l'*Hindenburg* savouraient leur cocktail glacé LZ 129 (du gin avec un peu de jus d'orange) avant de passer au « foie gras de caneton façon bavaroise accompagné de chou au champagne » ou bien aux « escalopes de gibier Beauval et pommes de terre Berny » tout en survolant l'océan. « Le *Graf Zeppelin* est bien plus que juste des machines, de la toile et de l'aluminium. Il a une âme. » déclara Lady Grace Drummond Hay. Mais l'âme du dirigeable fut détruite le 6 mai 1937 lorsque l'*Hindenburg* s'enflamma alors qu'il tentait d'atteindre le mât d'amarrage à Lakehurst, New Jersey. À peine quatorze ans plus tard, le *Comet* de De Havilland, le premier avion de ligne à réaction, prit son envol. À la fin des années cinquante, le transport aérien était devenu le moyen de transport intercontinental le plus rapide et le moins onéreux et menaçait de mettre fin à ses rivaux.

Ce ne fut pas le cas. L'enchantement lié aux voyages demeura sous toutes ses formes – la route, les chemins de fer, les bateaux et les avions. L'*Orient Express* ressuscita dans les années quatre-vingt-dix. À l'heure actuelle, on compte autant de bateaux de croisière traversant les mers qu'il y a cinquante ans. Chaque année, le ciel s'encombre davantage d'avions de ligne aérodynamiques transportant des voyageurs en quête de plaisir aux quatre coins du monde. Les moments magiques demeurent. Lorsque les derniers bagages sont casés dans le coffre de la voiture ou bien lorsque le sac à dos est jeté par dessus les épaules … en route pour le voyage.

BELOW

A thousand photos, a thousand memories – and all crammed into a few days. Japanese tourists capture some of London's pomp and ceremony as their coach drives along Whitehall, 16th September 1973.

OPPOSITE

Sun, snow and sophistication. After a tough day modelling the latest ski and apres ski outfits, an all-female party get together for an off-piste celebration in the 1950s.

UNTEN

Tausend Fotos, tausend Erinnerungen – und alles hineingepackt in wenige Tage. Japanische Touristen fangen während der Fahrt an Whitehall vorbei, Londons Pomp und Zeremonien ein (16. September 1973).

RECHTE SEITE

Sonne, Schnee und Eleganz. Nach einem harten Tag der Vorstellung der neuesten Ski- und Aprés-Ski-Mode trifft sich in den fünfziger Jahren eine Gruppe von Frauen zu einem Fest abseits der Piste.

EN BAS

Des milliers de photos, des milliers de souvenirs et tout cela accumulé en quelques jours. Des touristes japonais capturent au vol certains aspects du faste et des cérémonies londoniennes alors que leur car roule le long de Whitehall, 16 septembre 1973.

CI-CONTRE

Le soleil, la neige et l'ambiance sophistiquée. Après une dure journée de présentation des dernières collections de vêtements de ski et d'après-ski, un groupe de femmes se réunit pour une fête hors-piste dans les années cinquante.

TRAVELLERS
REISENDE
LES VOYAGEURS

TODAY'S TRAVELLERS are the fastest the world has ever known, for they can reach the other side of the world in less than a day – admittedly arriving gummy-eyed and short of sleep, in need of a wash, desperate for good tea or coffee. They are also better prepared than their wandering predecessors, for, in most cases, they will have already paid for their return flight, their hotel or apartment, and even some of their meals. They know where they will stay, for how long, what the place looks like, what facilities it has to offer. They know most of what lies in store.

It was not always so. Travellers in the 18th and early 19th centuries had scant idea of what they would find *en route* or at their journey's end, and could only guess at what it would cost. And, though they travelled of their own volition, they did not always appreciate what they found. Writers especially complained. Smollett declared Versailles 'dismal' and the entire Italian *campania* 'desolate and dismal'. Arthur Young hated French cooking and 'the abominable garlick'. Goethe so loathed Italian coaches that he got out and walked. Mark Twain was depressed by Venice, whose canals were polluted by 'puffing, gasping and clattering twopenny steamers'. Dr Johnson found the Highlands of Scotland intolerably monotonous, and Rousseau disliked every mountain he came across. Joseph Haydn longed to return to Vienna, for the noise of the 'common people of London was intolerable'. Others condemned the 'tide of prostitutes in Rome', with 'disorderly houses springing up like weeds in the night'.

But these tough and determined pioneers kept going, and their reports merely whetted the appetites of those that followed. The new breed saw the world through more romantic eyes. They were enthusiastic, appreciative of the works of man and nature, and critical only of their fellow-travellers. Lord Byron described Rome as 'pestilent with English…A man is a fool who travels now in France or Italy, till this tribe of wretches is swept home again'. The problem for his Lordship – and many others – was that travel had become too popular. In 1818, it was reckoned that there were 2,000 English in Rome and 30,000 in Paris. By 1840 there were 11,000 visitors a year to Florence, and from 1860 onwards 40,000 Americans crossed the Atlantic each year for what amounted to a new Grand Tour of Europe.

So the romantic and the adventurous – many of them women – sought wider horizons. Lady Hester Stanhope set out with her brother, her maid and her physician to Spain, Malta, Greece and Egypt – where she adopted the dress of a Turkish man. Mary Fitzgibbon spent two years in the freezing vastnesses of the Canadian Arctic. Crossing the United States by rail, Viscountess Avonmore risked her life as she traversed 'ledges so fearfully narrow that if one dropped a glove from the carriage window, it would have fallen straight three hundred feet'. The photographer John Thomson felt safer, and happier, in a Chinese opium den, 'with girls in constant attendance, some ready to prepare and charge the bowl of the pipe with opium and others

to sing sweet melodies to waft the sleeper off into dreamland…' In 1889, Elizabeth Cochrane adopted the name Nellie Bly, and set off in the footsteps of Phileas Fogg. It took her just seventy-two days to go round the world.

Travellers began to move in packs across the face of the globe. Academics took notebooks and cameras to Greece and Rome. Sweating sightseers hired charabancs to transport them across the sands of Egypt to the Sphinx and the Pyramids. Diplomats cooled themselves in the Spanish summer at cafes along the tree-lined *avenidas* of San Sebastien. Hunters roamed the forests of Eastern Europe in search of wild boar. Henriette d'Anguille followed many up Mont Blanc in 1838, taking with her a team of porters to carry two legs of mutton, two ox tongues, twenty-four fowls, eighteen bottles of 'good' wine, a cask of *vin ordinaire*, a bottle of brandy, and a supply of chocolate and French plums.

By the early 20th century, the adventurous were greatly outnumbered by the pleasure-seekers. The new traveller wanted sun and sea, cocktails and laughter. The athletic still roped themselves together to scale mountains. Invalids were still trundled from spa to spa. There were still culture-vultures in search of the glories of the Italian Renaissance or the marvels of German Gothic, but the new generation preferred the beaches of the French and Italian Rivieras. The trickle of travellers became a stream. Many came by train. A few

BELOW

Economy class passengers carry their own luggage on to the Cunard *White Star* liner *Queen Mary* at Southampton Docks, 27th May 1936. It was the great ship's maiden voyage to New York.

OPPOSITE

A hiking trio arrives at Waterloo Station, London, 1932. In the health-and-fitness conscious 1930s, hiking was one of the most popular leisure activities – whether a mere day's stroll on nearby downs or a fortnight's hard slogging in foreign lands.

UNTEN

Passagiere der *Economy Class* bringen ihr Gepäck selbst an Bord des *White Star* Liniendampfers *Queen Mary* von Cunard an den Docks von Southampton (27. Mai 1936). Es war die Jungfernfahrt des großartigen Schiffs nach New York.

LINKE SEITE

Ein Wanderertrio erreicht die Waterloo Station in London (1932). In den gesundheits- und fitnessbewussten dreißiger Jahren gehörte das Wandern zu den beliebtesten Freizeitaktivitäten – gleich ob bei einem Tagesspaziergang durch die benachbarten Hügel oder einer vierzehntägigen Plackerei in fremden Gefilden.

EN BAS

Des passagers de la classe touriste transportent eux-mêmes leur bagage sur le paquebot de ligne *Queen Mary* de la Cunard *White Star* aux docks de Southampton, 27 mai 1936. C'était le voyage inaugural de ce grand bateau à destination de New York.

CI-CONTRE

Un trio de marcheurs arrive à la gare de Waterloo, Londres, 1932. Dans les années trente, époque de prise de conscience dans le domaine de la santé et de la forme physique, la marche à pied était un des loisirs les plus populaires – que ce soit pour une simple balade d'un jour dans les alentours ou bien pour une marche harassante d'une quinzaine de jours dans un pays étranger.

daredevils flew in. Well-heeled Americans shipped their limousines from the States and drove down. The extravagantly wealthy dropped anchor from their private yachts in the dazzling waters of the Med. All that was needed to join in the fun was a bankroll of dollars, a *peignoir*, some sun cream and a dash of *joie de vivre*.

Across the world, film stars, politicians, princes and princesses, newspaper magnates and business tycoons, millionaires and industrialists journeyed together in cosseted bliss. Magazines published photographs and articles detailing the comings and goings of the famous on board ship, plane and train. To be seen playing deck tennis, waving from the tarmac of a runway, or boarding a beautiful train was enough to justify one's existence. To be *en voyage* was to be alive. Hedonism rather than curiosity now motivated the modern traveller.

These new-found joys came to an end in 1939, to reappear in less luxurious form in the late 1940s and 1950s. But another revolution was under way. It was fuelled by three innovations: the jet airliner, the package holiday, and the invention of a commodity known as 'leisure'. The jumbo jet made it possible to fly hundreds of people swiftly and cheaply to almost any part of the globe. The package holiday removed the need for people to plan their holidays and drastically reduced the cost of a week or two in the sun. Shorter work-

ing weeks and holidays with pay presented millions of workers with time and the opportunity to get away from it all. And the rapidly growing travel industry pointed them in the right directions.

By the 1960s the departure and arrival lounges of airports were packed with this new breed of traveller – the one- or two-week tourist. They carried fewer items of luggage than the pre-war traveller. They, too, were more interested in fun than famous architecture, but they preferred to export their own popular culture – anything from McDonalds and fish and chip shops, to discos and sliced bread. Twenty years later, a new generation of baseball-capped travellers took their culture and their families further afield, for there was sunshine and much else to be found on the beaches of Mexico, the Caribbean, Florida, south east Asia, Australia and southern Africa. More than that, there was an increasing number of places providing activities worth spending time and money to pursue – scuba-diving, surfing, deep-sea fishing, jet-skiing, para-gliding and many more.

The stream is now a flood, and the 21st century has already produced new species of traveller. There are those prepared and able to spend a fortune on a ticket to space itself. There are a few who have purchased permanent occupation of a cabin on a cruise ship and now live on board. For such people, travelling has become a way of life. And for the millions of others who check in for their flights, board their trains, or simply head for the nearest *autobahn*, *peage* or freeway, it is enough to be doing what many love above all else – travelling.

OPPOSITE

OPPOSITE
In a scene reminiscent of E. M. Forster's *Secret Life*, a tourist and guide reveal their friendship on a roof terrace in Tunisia, 1908.

BELOW
American tourists pause long enough to snap young inhabitants of Volendam, Holland in traditional costume, 9th August 1937.

LINKE SEITE
In einer Szene, die an E. M. Forsters *Secret Life* erinnert, enthüllen ein Tourist und ein Führer auf einer Dachterrasse in Tunesien ihre Freundschaft (1908).

UNTEN
Amerikanische Touristen legen eine kurze Pause ein, um junge Einwohner von Volendam, Holland, in ihren traditionellen Kostümen zu fotografieren (9. August 1937).

CI-CONTRE
Dans une scène qui rappelle *La vie secrète* de E. M. Forster, un touriste et un guide révèlent leur amitié sur la terrasse située sur un toit en Tunisie, 1908.

EN BAS
Des touristes américains font une pause suffisante pour pouvoir photographier des jeunes habitants de Volendam, Hollande en costumes traditionnels, 9 août 1937.

DIE HEUTIGEN REISENDEN sind die Schnellsten, die die Welt je gekannt hat, denn sie können in weniger als einem Tag die andere Seite der Welt erreichen – zugegebenermaßen mit rotgeränderten Augen, übermüdet und mit dem verzweifelten Wunsch nach einem Bad und einer guten Tasse Tee oder Kaffee. Sie sind außerdem besser vorbereitet als ihre wandernden Vorfahren, denn sie haben in den meisten Fällen bereits ihr Rückflugticket in der Tasche, ihr Hotel oder Apartment und sogar einige ihrer Mahlzeiten im Voraus bezahlt. Sie wissen, wo sie verweilen werden und wie lange, wie es an diesem Ort aussieht, welche Annehmlichkeiten er bietet. Sie wissen zumeist, was sie zu erwarten haben.

Das war nicht immer so. Reisende im 18. und frühen 19. Jahrhundert hatten nicht die geringste Ahnung, was sie unterwegs oder am Ende ihrer Reise erwarten würde und konnten nur schätzen, was es sie kosten würde. Außerdem gefiel ihnen nicht immer, was sie zu sehen bekamen, auch dann, wenn sie aus freiem Willen reisten. Besonders Schriftsteller gaben sich kritisch. Smollet beschrieb Versailles als „düster" und die gesamte italienische *Campania* als „trostlos und trist". Arthur Young hasste die französische Küche und „den grässlichen Knoblauch". Goethe verabscheute die italienischen Kutschen so sehr, dass er ausstieg und zu Fuß ging. Mark Twain war von Venedig deprimiert, dessen Kanäle von „qualmenden, keuchenden und klappernden Billigdampfern" verpestet wurden. Dr. Johnson befand die schottischen Highlands für unerträglich

On a spring day in 1972, visitors hurry through the beautifully restored sights of the town of Goslar in Southern Lower Saxony, on the northern edge of the Harz mountains. They have much to see in the town that was once 'the treasure chest of the Holy Roman Empire'

BELOW

Sunshine, fresh sea air, and (in the case of at least one of the party) a refreshing cigarette… A classic pose for the camera on a day trip to Eastbourne, Sussex, 5th June 1930.

An einem Frühlingstag im Jahr 1972 eilen Besucher durch die herrlich restaurierte Altstadt Goslars im südlichen Niedersachsen, am Nordrand des Harzes. Die einstige „Schatztruhe des Heiligen Römischen Reiches" bietet viele Sehenswürdigkeiten.

UNTEN

Sonnenschein, frische Meeresbrise und (zumindest für einen in der Gruppe) ein Zug aus der Zigarette... Eine klassische Kamerapose während eines Tagesausflugs nach Eastbourne, Sussex, England (5. Juni 1930).

Par un jour de printemps de 1972, les visiteurs se pressent dans la ville magnifiquement restaurée de Goslar, au sud de la Basse Saxe, à l'extrémité nord des montagnes du Harz. Ils ont beaucoup à voir dans la ville qui fut autrefois « le coffre au trésor du Saint Empire romain germanique».

EN BAS

Un rayon de soleil, l'air frais de la mer et (c'est le cas d'au moins une personne du groupe) une cigarette rafraîchissante … Une pause classique pour l'appareil-photo lors d'une excursion d'un jour à Eastbourne, Sussex, 5 juin 1930.

Though much impeded by their Victorian dress, a mixed party of travellers steps boldly out to cross the Chamonix Glacier in the Savoy Alps, 1867.

Trotz der Behinderung durch die viktorianische Kleidung macht sich eine gemischte Reisegruppe mutig auf, den Chamonix-Gletscher in den Savoyer Alpen zu überqueren (1867).

Bien qu'ils soient très gênés par leurs vêtements de l'époque victorienne, un groupe mixte de voyageurs sort hardiment pour traverser le glacier de Chamonix dans les Alpes de Savoie, 1867.

eintönig und Rousseau hatte eine Abneigung gegenüber jedem Berg, den er überquerte. Joseph Haydn sehnte sich nach Wien zurück, denn für ihn war der Krach der „gemeinen Leute in London unerträglich". Andere verurteilten „die Flut von Prostituierten in Rom", wo „Freudenhäuser wie Unkraut aus der Erde schossen".

Doch diese harten und entschlossenen Pioniere reisten weiter und ihre Berichte machten ihren Nachfolgern nur noch mehr Appetit. Die neue Spezies sah die Welt mit eher romantischen Augen. Sie war enthusiastisch und wusste die Werke des Menschen und der Natur zu schätzen. Kritisch war sie nur gegenüber ihren Reisekollegen. Lord Byron beschrieb Rom als „von Engländern verseucht... ein Mann, der jetzt nach Frankreich und Italien reist, ist verrückt, wenn er nicht wartet, bis diese Gattung von Blödmännern wieder nach Hause geschwemmt worden ist." Das Problem seiner Lordschaft – und vieler anderer – war, dass das Reisen zu beliebt geworden war. Im Jahr 1818, so schätzte man, hielten sich 2.000 Engländer in Rom und 30.000 in Paris auf. 1840 besuchten 11.000 Reisende jährlich Florenz und von 1860 an überquerten pro Jahr 40.000 Amerikaner den Atlantik, was mit einer neuen *Grand Tour* in Europa gleichzusetzen war.

So suchten die Romantiker und Abenteurer – darunter viele Frauen – fernere Horizonte. Lady Hester Stanhope machte sich zusammen mit ihrem Bruder, ihrem Dienstmädchen sowie ihrem Leibarzt auf den Weg nach Spanien, Malta, Griechenland und Ägypten – wo sie sich wie ein türkischer Mann kleidete. Mary Fitzgibbon verbrachte zwei Jahre in der klirrend kalten Weite der kanadischen Arktis. Auf ihrer Zugreise durch die Vereinigten Staaten riskierte die Viscountess Avonmore ihr Leben, als sie Felsklippen überquerte „so furchterregend schmal, dass ein Handschuh, den man zum Wagenfenster hinauswerfen würde, glatt hundert Meter in die Tiefe fiele". Der Fotograf John Thomson fühlte sich sicherer (und glücklicher) in einer chinesischen Opiumhöhle, „mit Mädchen in ständiger Bereitschaft. Einige, um die Pfeife mit Opium zu stopfen, andere, um süße Melodien zu singen, die den Schläfer ins Traumland tragen..." Im Jahr 1889 nahm Elizabeth Cochrane den Namen Nellie Bly an und begab sich in die Fußstapfen von Phileas Fogg. Sie benötigte nur zweiundsiebzig Tage, um die Welt zu umrunden.

Reisende begannen, in Horden über den Globus zu ziehen. Akademiker reisten mit Notizbuch und Kamera nach Griechenland und Rom. Schwitzende Touristen mieteten offene Busse, die sie durch den Sand Ägyptens zur Sphinx und den Pyramiden bringen sollten. Diplomaten erfrischten sich im spanischen Sommer in den Cafés entlang der baumgesäumten *Avenidas* von San Sebastian. Jäger durchstreiften die Wälder Osteuropas auf der Suche nach wilden Ebern. Henriette d'Anguille folgten 1838 viele auf den Mont Blanc. Sie nahm zwei Trägermannschaften mit, die zwei Hammelkeulen, zwei Ochsenzungen, vierundzwanzig Hühner, achtzehn Flaschen „guten Wein", ein Fass *Vin ordinaire*, eine Flasche Brandy und einen Vorrat an Schokolade und französischen Pflaumen schleppten.

Im frühen zwanzigsten Jahrhundert wurden die Abenteurer von den Vergnügungssuchenden zahlenmäßig weit übertroffen. Der neue Reisende wollte Sonne und Meer, Cocktails und Spaß. Die Athleten bildeten noch immer Seilschaften, um Berge zu erklimmen. Kranke wurden noch immer von Heilbad zu Heilbad gerollt. Es gab noch immer Kulturversessene auf der Suche nach der Pracht der italienischen Renaissance oder den Wundern der deutschen Gotik, doch die neue Generation bevorzugte die Strände der französischen und italienischen Riviera. Das Rinnsal der Reisenden wurde zum Strom. Viele kamen mit dem Zug. Ein paar Waghalsige flogen ein. Gut betuchte Amerikaner brachten auf dem Schiff ihre Limousinen mit und fuhren selbst die Küsten entlang. Die verschwenderischen Wohlhabenden ankerten mit ihren Privatjachten auf dem glitzernden Wasser des Mittelmeers. Alles, was nötig war, um bei diesem Spaß dabei zu sein, waren ein Bündel Dollarnoten, ein Negligee, etwas Sonnencreme und eine *Prise Joie de vivre*.

OPPOSITE

The famous Russian ballerina Anna Pavlova at the Pyramids,
September 1923. The discovery of Tutankhamen's tomb ten
months earlier had sparked off an outbreak of 'Egyptomania'
which was to last for the next few years.

RIGHT

Heading for the pale blue yonder. A young woman smiles for
the camera of Slim Aarons before embarking on the thrills of
paragliding above Acapulco, 1968.

LINKE SEITE

Die berühmte russische Ballerina Anna Pavlova bei den
Pyramiden (September 1923). Die Entdeckung des Grabes
von Tutenchamun zehn Monate zuvor löste eine wahre
„Ägyptomanie" aus, die die nächsten Jahre anhalten sollte.

RECHTS

Start in den blassblauen Himmel. Eine junge Frau lächelt für
Slim Aarons in die Kamera, bevor sie zu einem aufregenden
Paragliding-Flug über Acapulco abhebt (1968).

CI-CONTRE

La fameuse ballerine russe Anna Pavlova visite les Pyramides,
septembre 1923. La découverte de la tombe de Toutânkha-
mon dix mois plus tôt a déclenché une vague d' égyptomanie
qui devait durer quelques années encore.

A DROITE

En route pour le ciel bleu. Une jeune femme souriante pose
pour la photo de Slim Aarons avant de goûter aux sensations
du parapente au dessus d' Acapulco, 1968.

ABOVE

Students from Canada, the United States, Germany and Sweden prepare for a night's sleep in the *Southwark College of Education*, 16th August 1970. The accommodation cost them 30p each per night, and had been arranged by the London Tourist Office to cope with the August rush of visitors.

OPPOSITE

In the mid-1950s hitchhikers offer a variety of destinations to passing motorists – MUNICH, HEIDELBERG, STUTTGART AND HANNOVER being among their preferred locations. Where they eventually ended up is anyone's guess.

OBEN

Studentinnen aus Kanada, den Vereinigten Staaten, Deutschland und Schweden bereiten sich auf eine Übernachtung im *Southwark College of Education* vor (16. August 1970). Die Unterkunft kostet sie 30 Pence pro Nacht und wurde vom Londoner Touristenbüro arrangiert, um dem sommerlichen Besuchersturm Herr zu werden.

RECHTE SEITE

Mitte der fünziger Jahre halten Tramper den vorbeifahrenden Autos eine Auswahl an Schildern entgegen – MÜNCHEN, HEIDELBERG, STUTTGART UND HANNOVER gehörten zu ihren bevorzugten Zielen. Wo sie letztlich ankamen, lässt sich lediglich raten.

EN HAUT

Des étudiants du Canada, des États-Unis, de l'Allemagne et de la Suède se préparent à passer la nuit au *Southwark College of Education*, 16 août 1970. Le logement coûte à chacun 30 pence par nuit et a dû être organisé par l'office du tourisme de Londres en raison de l'arrivée massive de touristes du mois d'août.

CI-CONTRE

Au milieu des années cinquante, les auto-stoppeurs offrent une variété de destinations aux automobilistes qui croisent leur route – MUNICH, HEIDELBERG, STUTTGART ET HANNOVRE étant parmi les endroits favoris. Reste à savoir où ils aboutiront vraiment.

Überall auf der Welt trafen Filmstars, Politiker, Prinzen und Prinzessinnen, Zeitungsmagnaten und Businesstycoons, Millionäre und Industrielle in verwöhnter Glückseligkeit aufeinander. Zeitschriften veröffentlichten Fotos und Artikel über das Kommen und Gehen der Berühmtheiten an Bord von Schiffen, Flugzeugen und Eisenbahnen. Beim Decktennis, winkend auf dem Asphalt einer Landebahn oder beim Besteigen eines wunderschönen Zuges gesehen zu werden war genug, um die eigene Existenz zu rechtfertigen. Auf Reisen zu sein, hieß zu leben. Mehr Hedonismus als Neugier war nun für moderne Reisende die Motivation.

Diese neuen Freuden fanden 1939 ein jähes Ende und tauchten Ende der vierziger und in den fünfziger Jahren in weniger luxuriöser Form wieder auf, doch da war bereits eine neue Revolution im Anmarsch. Sie wurde von drei Innovationen getrieben: Dem Düsenjet, dem Pauschalurlaub und der Erfindung der Ware „Freizeit". Der Jumbojet machte es möglich, Hunderte von Menschen schnell und preiswert zu fast jedem Ort der Erde zu fliegen. Der Pauschalurlaub ersetzte die Notwendigkeit zur eigenen Urlaubsplanung und reduzierte die Kosten für ein oder zwei Wochen in der Sonne drastisch. Kürzere Wochenarbeitszeiten und bezahlter Urlaub boten Millionen von Arbeitnehmern die Zeit und die finanzielle Möglichkeit, einmal alles hinter sich zu lassen, und die rasch wachsende Reiseindustrie wies allen die richtigen Wege.

In den sechziger Jahren waren die Ankunfts- und Abflughallen der Flughäfen voll dieser neuen Gattung von Reisenden – den Ein- oder Zwei-Wochen-Touristen. Sie hatten weniger Gepäck als die Reisenden vor 1939 und sie waren mehr an Spaß als an berühmter Architektur interessiert. Sie zogen es vor, ihre eigene geliebte Kultur zu exportieren – von McDonalds und Fish-and-Chips-Buden bis hin zu Diskotheken und Scheibenbrot. Zwanzig Jahre später brachte eine neue Generation Reisender mit Baseballmützen ihre Kultur und ihre Familien in weiter entfernte Gegenden, wo Sonnenschein und vieles mehr zu finden war: An die Strände von Mexiko, der Karibik, Florida, Südostasien, Australien und Südafrika. Mehr noch: Es gab eine wachsende Anzahl von Orten, die Aktivitäten boten, in die man gerne Zeit und Geld investierte – Tauchen, Surfen, Tiefseefischen, Jetskiing, Paragliding und vieles mehr.

Heute ist der Strom zur Flut geworden und das 21. Jahrhundert hat wiederum eine neue Spezies von Reisenden hervorgebracht. Da sind jene, die ein Vermögen aufbringen können und wollen, um ins All zu fliegen. Es gibt ein paar, die sich eine Unterkunft auf einem Kreuzfahrtschiff gekauft haben und nun an Bord leben. Für diese Menschen ist das Reisen zu einem Lebensstil geworden. Für jene Millionen, die zu ihrem Flug einchecken, ihren Zug besteigen oder einfach in Richtung der nächsten Autobahn, Mautstrecke oder Freeway aufbrechen, ist es genug, das zu tun, was viele über alles lieben – reisen.

LES VOYAGEURS D'AUJOURD'HUI sont les plus rapides que le monde ait jamais connus puisque ils peuvent aller à l'autre bout du monde en moins d'un jour. Certes ils arrivent avec des yeux cernés par manque de sommeil, ils ont besoin d'une douche et d'un bon thé ou d'un café fort. Ils sont aussi mieux préparés que leurs prédécesseurs puisque, dans la plupart des cas, ils ont déjà payé leur voyage du retour, leur hôtel ou appartement et même quelques repas. Ils savent où ils vont rester et pour combien de temps, à quoi ressemble l'endroit où ils se trouvent et quels en sont les diverses installations. Ils savent la plupart du temps à quoi s'attendre.

Ce n'était pas toujours le cas. Les voyageurs du 18ème et du début du 19ème siècle n'avaient pas beaucoup d'idées sur ce qu'ils trouveraient en route ou à la fin de leur voyage et pouvaient seulement deviner ce que cela allait leur coûter. De plus, bien qu'ils voyageaient de leur gré, ils n'appréciaient pas toujours ce qu'ils trouvaient. Les écrivains, en particulier, se lamentaient. Smollett a déclaré que Versailles était « lugubre » et que la *Campanie* italienne était « triste et désolée ». Arthur Young détestait la cuisine française et son « ail abominable ». Goethe avait les calèches italiennes tellement en horreur qu'il descendait et préférait marcher. Mark Twain était déprimé par Venise dont les canaux étaient pollués par « des bateaux à vapeur de quatre sous envoyant des bouffées de fumée, suffoquant et cliquetant ». Le Docteur Johnson trouvait les

BELOW

Rubbing the eyes. A slight difficulty in focussing for father and child while on holiday in Indonesia.

OPPOSITE

Two British hitchhikers on the last lap of their bargain journey from London to St Tropez on the French Riviera. They featured in a *Picture Post* article called 'We Hitchhiked to the Sun for £5' in July 1954.

UNTEN

Da muss man sich die Augen reiben. Leichte Schwierigkeiten beim Fokusieren für Vater und Kind bei einem Urlaub in Indonesien.

LINKE SEITE

Zwei britische Tramperinnen auf der letzten Etappe ihrer Billigreise von London nach St. Tropez an der französischen Riviera. Sie waren Thema eines Bildberichts in der *Picture Post* mit dem Titel „Wir trampten für 5 Pfund in die Sonne" (Juli 1954).

EN BAS

En train de se frotter les yeux. Mise au point difficile pour le père et l'enfant lors de vacances en Indonésie.

CI-CONTRE

Deux auto-stoppeuses britanniques lors de la dernière étape de leur voyage à bon marché de Londres à Saint-Tropez sur la Côte d'Azur. Elles figurent dans un article du *Picture Post* intitulé « Nous allons au soleil en auto-stop pour 5 livres sterling » en juillet 1954.

Highlands d'Écosse absolument monotones et Rousseau détestait chaque montagne qu'il croisait sur son chemin. Joseph Haydn désirait rentrer à Vienne car « le bruit des gens du commun à Londres était intolérable ». D'autres condamnaient la « marée de prostituées à Rome » avec « ses maisons de débauche poussant comme des mauvaises herbes pendant la nuit ».

Toutefois ces pionniers résistants et déterminés continuèrent de voyager et leurs rapports ne faisaient que stimuler davantage la soif de voyage de ceux qui les suivaient. La nouvelle race de voyageurs voyait le monde sous un angle plus romantique. Ils étaient plus enthousiastes, appréciaient davantage les œuvres de l'homme et de la nature et critiquaient uniquement leurs compagnons de voyage. Lord Byron décrivit Rome comme : « empestée d'anglais…Les hommes sont fous de voyager maintenant en France ou en Italie aussi longtemps que cette bande de misérables n'est pas rentrée à la maison. » Le problème pour ces Lords – et pour beaucoup d'autres – était que voyager était devenu trop populaire. En 1818, on estimait que 2.000 anglais étaient à Rome, 30.000 à Paris. En 1840, on comptait 11.000 visiteurs à Florence par an et à partir de 1860, 40.000 américains traversaient chaque année l'Atlantique pour ce qui allait devenir un nouveau Grand Tour d'Europe.

Ainsi les romantiques et les aventuriers – la plupart d'entre eux des femmes – recherchèrent des horizons plus vastes. Lady Hester Stanhope partit avec son frère, sa servante et son médecin en Espagne, à Malte, en Grèce et en Égypte – où elle s'habilla comme un homme turc. Mary Fitzgibbon passa deux ans dans les endroits glacés les plus reculés de l'Arctique canadien. Traversant les États-Unis par chemins de fer, la Vicomtesse Avonmore risqua la vie alors qu'elle passait sur « des saillies si dangereusement étroites que si quelqu'un laissait tomber un gant par la fenêtre du wagon, celui-ci tomberait 100 m plus bas ». Le photographe

CLOCKWISE FROM OPPOSITE
Young tourists recover from the fatigue of travel on a summer day in the Vondelpark, Amsterdam, 14th July 1971; A poster illustrating some of the more innocent delights of a *Club 18-30* holiday; Aqua maids from the famous Cypress Gardens water-ski show take a break on a Florida beach on a winter's day in 1979.

LINKE SEITE BEGINNEND IM UHRZEIGERSINN
Junge Touristen erholen sich von der ermüdenden Reise an einem Sommertag im Vondelpark, Amsterdam (14. Juli 1971); Ein Plakat wirbt mit den eher unschuldigen Freuden eines Urlaubs im *Club 18-30*; Die jungen Frauen der berühmten Wasserski-Show von Cypress Gardens machen an einem Wintertag an einem Strand in Florida Pause (1979).

DANS LE SENS DES AIGUILLES D'UNE MONTRE, A PARTIR DE LA PHOTO CI-CONTRE
Des jeunes touristes se remettent de la fatigue du voyage au Vondelpark, Amsterdam par un beau jour d'été, 14 juillet 1971. Un poster illustre quelques plaisirs parmi les plus innocents des vacances du *club 18–30*. Les jeunes filles figurant dans le fameux show de ski nautique de Cypress Gardens font une pause sur une plage de Floride un jour d'hiver de 1979.

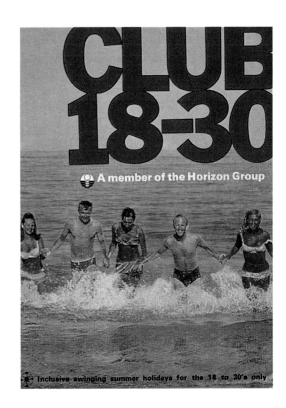

LEFT
Facing the sun, but well
wrapped up against the
cold, a party of winter holidaymakers enjoy the restful
delights of Gstaad,
Switzerland, March 1961.

OPPOSITE
Sunbathing, factory style.
Catherine Wilke sips her
Coke before taking her
place on the shelves of
Capri in August 1980. Both
photographs were taken by
Slim Aarons.

LINKS
Das Gesicht der Sonne zu-
gewandt, doch gut ein-
gepackt gegen die Kälte
genießt eine Gruppe Win-
terurlauber die erholsamen
Freuden von Gstaadt,
Schweiz (März 1961).

RECHTE SEITE
Fabrikartiges Sonnenbad.
Catherine Wilks trinkt eine
Cola bevor sie ihren Platz
auf den regalähnlichen
Sonnenbänken auf Capri
einnimmt (August 1980).
Beide Aufnahmen sind von
Slim Aarons.

A GAUCHE
Exposés au soleil, mais bien
emmitouflés contre le froid,
un groupe de vacanciers
d'hiver profitent des
charmes paisibles de
Gstaad, Suisse, mars 1961.

CI-CONTRE
Bain de soleil comme dans
une usine. Catherine Wilke
sirote son coca avant de
prendre place sur les
étagères de Capri en août
1980. Les deux photos ont
été prises par Slim Aarons.

John Thompson se sentait plus en sécurité et plus heureux dans une fumerie d'opium avec « des filles constamment à son service, certaines pour préparer et mettre l'opium dans le récipient du tuyau et d'autres pour fredonner des mélodies tellement douces qu'elles vous font plonger dans le monde des songes ». En 1889, Élisabeth Cochrane adopta le nom de Nellie Bly et suivit les traces de Phileas Fogg. Il ne lui fallut que soixante-douze jours pour faire le tour du monde.

Les voyageurs se mirent à traverser le globe. Les universitaires prenaient des carnets et des appareils photo pour aller en Grèce et à Rome. Des touristes en sueurs louaient des cars décapotables pour les transporter dans le désert d'Égypte jusqu'au Sphinx et aux Pyramides. Sous le soleil d'Espagne, les diplomates se rafraîchissaient dans des cafés le long des *avenidas* bordées d'arbres de Saint Sébastien. Les chasseurs parcouraient les forêts de l'Europe de l'Est en quête de sangliers sauvages. Henriette d'Anguille suivit beaucoup de prédécesseurs au sommet du Mont Blanc en 1838, emmenant avec elle une équipe de porteurs pour transporter deux pattes de moutons, deux langues de bœuf, vingt-quatre volailles, dix-huit bouteilles de bon vin, un fût de vin ordinaire, une bouteille de brandy et une réserve de chocolat et de prunes françaises.

Au début du vingtième siècle, les touristes en quête de plaisir surpassaient largement les aventuriers. Les nouveaux voyageurs voulaient le soleil et la mer, les cocktails et l'amusement. Les plus sportifs continuaient

OPPOSITE

The Italian Princess Luciana Pignatelli checks her skis before setting off down the piste near Lech, Austria in February 1961. At that time, skiing was still predominantly a pastime limited to the well-to-do.

RIGHT

A generation later, the number of skiers had dramatically increased, as had the number of ski resorts around the world to cope with the crowds who insisted on their right to break a leg, even in a snowstorm.

LINKE SEITE

Die italienische Prinzessin Luciana Pignatelli überprüft ihre Ski, bevor sie die Abfahrt in der Nähe von Lech in Österreich in Angriff nimmt (Februar 1961). Zu dieser Zeit war das Skifahren vor allem ein Zeitvertreib der Gutsituierten.

RECHTS

Eine Generation später hat sich die Anzahl der Skifahrer drastisch erhöht, ebenso die Zahl der Skigebiete auf der ganzen Welt, die die Massen derer aufnehmen, die auf ihr Recht bestehen, sich selbst bei Schneesturm ein Bein brechen zu dürfen.

CI-CONTRE

La princesse italienne Luciana Pignatelli contrôle ses skis avant de s'élancer sur les pistes de Lech, Autriche en février 1961. À cette époque, le ski était un loisir principalement réservé aux nantis.

A DROITE

Une génération plus tard, le nombre de skieurs a considérablement augmenté tout comme le nombre de stations de sports d'hiver dans le monde pour pouvoir accueillir les foules qui revendiquent le droit de se casser une jambe, même en pleine tempête de neige.

BELOW

A motorcycle and sidecar, a small tent, a banjolele, a wind-up gramophone and a folding camera – all that was needed for an unforgettable tour through darkest Surrey in south east England in the mid-1920s.

OPPOSITE

Fifty years later, the well-equipped camper carried considerably more gear. Two young boys escape from it all on the shores of Lake Balaton, Hungary, July 1974.

UNTEN

Ein Motorrad mit Beiwagen, ein kleines Zelt, ein Banjo, ein Gramofon und eine Faltkamera – dies war alles, was für eine unvergessliche Tour durchs hinterste Surrey im Südosten Englands Mitte der zwanziger Jahre nötig war.

RECHTE SEITE

Fünfzig Jahre später geht der gut ausgestattete Camper mit erheblich mehr Ausrüstung auf Reisen. Zwei kleine Jungen suchen am Plattensee in Ungarn, Erholung (Juli 1974).

EN BAS

Une moto et un side-car, une petite tente, un banjo, un gramophone, un appareil-photo pliant – tout cela était nécessaire pour une excursion inoubliable dans le sombre Surrey au sud-est de l'Angleterre au milieu des années vingt.

CI-CONTRE

Cinquante ans plus tard, le camping-car bien équipé peut transporter beaucoup plus de matériel. Deux jeunes garçons se reposent dans leur abri sur les rives du lac Balaton en Hongrie, juillet 1974.

à s'encorder pour escalader les montagnes. Les invalides étaient toujours transportés de termes en termes. Les passionnés de culture continuaient leur quête des gloires de la renaissance italienne ou des merveilles du gothique allemand, mais les nouvelles générations préféraient la Côte d'Azur et la Riviera italienne. Les quelques voyageurs d'autrefois devinrent un flux de voyageurs. De nombreux touristes arrivaient en train. Quelques audacieux prenaient l'avion. Les nantis américains embarquaient aussi leur limousine et roulaient vers le Sud. Les incroyablement riches jetaient l'ancre de leur yacht privé dans les eaux transparentes de la Méditerranée. Tout ce qu'il fallait pour s'amuser était une liasse de dollars, un peignoir, de la crème solaire et un peu de joie de vivre.

Les acteurs, les politiciens, les princes et princesses, les magnats de la presse, les importants hommes d'affaires, les millionnaires et les industriels voyageaient à travers le monde dans un bonheur absolu. Les magazines publiaient des photographies et des articles détaillant les allées et venues des personnalités à bord d'avions, de trains ou de bateaux. Il suffisait d'être vu en train de jouer au tennis sur le pont d'un bateau ou de faire signe sur le tarmac d'un aéroport ou encore de monter sur un train prestigieux pour justifier sa propre existence. Être en voyage signifiait être en vie. L'hédonisme, plus que la curiosité, motivait maintenant le voyageur moderne.

OPPOSITE

Staff on a works outing to Margate enjoy the bouncy fun of the 'lilo' or floating bed, 4th September 1934. By the 1930s most such trips to the seaside were an annual event.

BELOW

Berliners practice the latest dance craze on the sands of the Wansee resort, 1925. It was the age of Surrealism, jazz and risqué revues, but it was still possible to get away for an hour or two of innocent fun by the lakeside.

LINKE SEITE

Mitarbeiter bei einem Betriebsausflug nach Margate haben Spaß mit der Luftmatratze (4. September 1934). Die meisten solcher Ausflüge ans Meer waren zu jener Zeit jährlich wiederkehrende Ereignisse.

UNTEN

Berliner üben am Wannsee-Strand die neuesten Tanzschritte (1925). Es war das Zeitalter des Surrealismus, des Jazz und der gewagten Revuen, doch es war immer noch möglich, für ein oder zwei Stunden unschuldigen Spaß am See zu genießen.

CI-CONTRE

Les employés d'une usine sortant à Margate profitent du plaisir de rebondir sur le « lilo » ou lit flottant, 4 septembre 1934. Dans les années trente, la plupart de ces excursions constituaient un événement annuel.

UNTEN

Les Berlinois s'adonnent à la dernière danse en vogue sur le sable de la station balnéaire de Wansee, 1925. C'était l'époque du surréalisme, du jazz et des revues osées, mais il était toujours possible de s'évader pour quelques heures de plaisir innocent au bord du lac.

Several hundred miles away, on the shores of the North Sea, Max Heimann and his fiancé burrow into the sand of a Dutch beach in the mid 1950s. Whether they were just having fun or desperately seeking protection from an off-sea breeze is unknown.

BELOW

Travellers and holiday-makers have become considerably more uninhibited over the years. This group of besmeared excursionists were photographed at Ilica, on the Turkish shores of the Aegean Sea, following an afternoon's muddy fun.

Mehrere hundert Kilometer weiter, an der Nordsee, buddeln Max Heimann und seine Verlobte im Sand eines holländischen Strandes (Mitte der fünfziger Jahre). Ob sie einfach nur Spaßes halber gruben oder verzweifelt Schutz vor einer heftigen Meeresbrise suchten, ist unbekannt.

UNTEN

Reisende und Urlauber sind im Laufe der Jahre zunehmend hemmungsloser geworden. Diese Gruppe schmutzstarrender Ausflügler wurden in Ilica, an der türkischen Ägäis-Küste, nach einem lustigen Nachmittag im Schlamm fotografiert.

À plusieurs centaines de kilomètres de là, sur les côtes de la Mer du Nord, Max Heimann et sa fiancée creusent le sable d'une plage hollandaise au milieu des années cinquante. La photo ne dit pas s'ils étaient seulement en train de s'amuser ou bien s'ils essayaient de se protéger de la brise du littoral.

EN BAS

Avec le temps, les voyageurs et les vacanciers sont devenus considérablement moins inhibés. Ce groupe d'excursionnistes barbouillés fut photographié à Llica sur les côtes turques de la Mer Égée à la fin d'un après-midi de divertissement « boueux ».

CLOCKWISE FROM OPPOSITE RIGHT
An 1930s advertisement for *Zon* sun-bathing oil promises to make its users 'a glorious brown' and to cure the bites of midges; Overcooked torsos line up at a campsite bar on Corfu in the late 1950s; Far more comfortable than a deck chair, but much more difficult to erect in a strong wind, the hammock deck chair was the rage of at the lidos back in July 1936.

IM UHRZEIGERSINN BEGINNEND BEIM RECHTEN BILD AUF DER LINKEN SEITE
Eine Reklame aus den dreißiger Jahren für *Zon* Sonnenöl verspricht dem Benutzer „eine herrliche Bräune" und Schutz vor Mückenstichen; Sonnen-verbrannte Torsi an einer Camping-platzbar auf Korfu (Ende der fünfziger Jahre); viel bequemer als ein Liegestuhl, doch noch schwerer aufzustellen bei starkem Wind. Die Hängemattenliege war 1936 an den Lidos der letzte Schrei.

DANS LE SENS DES AIGUILLES D'UNE MONTRE, A PARTIR DE LA PHOTO CI-CONTRE A DROITE
Une publicité de 1930 pour l'huile solaire *Zon* promet à ses utilisateurs un bronzage fascinant et un remède contre les piqûres de moucherons. Des torses brûlés par le soleil sont alignés au bar d'un camping à Corfou à la fin des années cinquante. Bien plus confortable qu'un transat, mais plus difficile à monter par grand vent, ce lit-hamac faisait fureur sur les lidos en juillet 1936.

CLOCKWISE FROM LEFT

Seeking shade by the Sphinx; Avoiding nemesis in Majorca
1932 – the poster warns against lewdness, lust and impudence
while on holiday; Finding oblivion in Ibiza, September 1984.

IM UHRZEIGERSINN VON LINKS

Schattensuche bei der Sphinx; Um gerechte Strafe auf
Mallorca zu vermeiden (1932) – warnt das Plakat vor
Anstößigkeit, Wollust und Dreistigkeit im Urlaub; Vergessen
finden auf Ibiza (September 1984).

DANS LE SENS DES AIGUILLES D'UNE MONTRE, A PARTIR DE
LA GAUCHE

À la recherche d'ombre près du Sphinx. Éviter la vengeance
de Némésis à Majorque en 1932 – le poster met en garde contre la lubricité, le désir et l'impudence pendant les vacances.
Comment trouver l'oubli à Ibiza, septembre 1984.

Foreigners or Savages?

WOE TO IMPURE CITIES! **WOE TO IMPURE COUNTRIES!**

GOD SEVERELY CHASTISES CORRUPTED CITIES

THE DELUGE   THE DEAD SEA

ARE PERENNIAL THREATS TO WORSHIPPERS OF THE FLESH.

MAJORCANS!

In contrast with the extreme courteousness and proverbial courtesy of so many foreigners who now and at all times have honoured us with their visit, is the behaviour of a strange hordes of savages that, naked of apparel and dignity and scorning our generosity and friendly hospitality, invade the streets and roads of our towns and villages, our hotels, our beaches, and the terraces of our houses, as though they wished to convert our Golden Isle, bathed in pure sunshine, into brothel of their vices and ground reserved for their nudity and scandalous exhibitions.

A QUICK REACTION MUST BE MADE

Because impudence and lust have sallied forth from their hiding places and, like covetous wild beasts, are preying upon our children and young people, and even upon full-grown men...

Such idolaters of sensualism, who rather than men would be animals, must be advised in some way or another that in Majorca virtue and decency are not bought with dollars or marks, nor any other foreign money.

WOE TO HIM WHO SCANDALIZES CHILDREN!

For the welfare of our children and young folk, who are the hope of the nation, the seed of the race and the future citizens of an immaculate country, we must ASK, EXACT and COMPEL that our usages and customs, which are those of a civilized land, be respected.

We are not a territory to conquer.

In return for our hospitality, we do not want to be bothered nor offended with carnivalesque attire and insolent nudities.

God expelled from Paradise our first parents

because they were considered unworthy to tread that virgin soil.

MAJORCA

has a sky too pure for such lewd people and a land too virgin for such corrupted and corruptive... immigrant Eves.

And this is our pride and this is our honour:

that we will not let ourselves be won over by anything or anybody whatsoever.

Africa has propitious shores to tan the skin of those who in order to cultivate the hygiene of the body have forgotten the health of the soul.

PALMA, EL TERRENO, SOLLER, POLLENSA...

towns and villages of Majorca, who to the beauty of your beaches and the charm of your flower-gardens join the mildness of your character and the attractiveness of your tempered habits,

for the safeguard of your dignity and that of your sons

united in firm, co-ordinate action, let us cooperate with the efforts of our first Civil Authority.

LET US ALL JOIN

in making known to the unscrupulous that Majorca is not a theatre in which to stage their clownish Carnival nor is there here a suitable place for lewd voracity and orgies.

Ces joies toutes nouvelles cessèrent en 1939 pour réapparaître sous des formes moins luxueuses à la fin des années quarante et dans les années cinquante. Toutefois une autre révolution était en cours. Elle fut provoquée par trois innovations : l'avion à réaction, les vacances organisées et l'invention d'un nouveau produit appelé « loisir ». Le Jumbo Jet permit de transporter des centaines de personnes rapidement et à bon marché vers presque tous les endroits du monde. Les vacances organisées permettaient de passer une semaine ou deux au soleil à coût réduit et rendaient la planification des vacances quasi superflue. La réduction du temps de travail et les congés payés offraient du temps libre aux travailleurs et les moyens de pouvoir s'évader pour quelques temps. L'industrie du tourisme croissait rapidement et emmenait ces voyageurs dans les bonnes directions.

Dans les années soixante, les halls de départ et d'arrivée des aéroports étaient remplis de cette nouvelle espèce de voyageurs – les touristes d'une ou deux semaines. Ils transportaient beaucoup moins de bagages que les voyageurs de l'avant-guerre. Eux aussi étaient plus intéressés par le plaisir que par les monuments célèbres et ils préféraient exporter leurs traditions populaires – des McDonalds aux *Fish and Chip*, des discothèques au pain en tranches. Vingt ans plus tard, une nouvelle génération de touristes coiffés de casquettes de base-ball emmenaient leurs familles et exportaient leur culture dans des pays plus lointains. En effet, on pouvait trouver le soleil et beaucoup plus encore sur les plages du Mexique, des Caraïbes, de Floride, du Sud-Est de l'Asie, de l'Australie et du Sud de l'Afrique. Bien plus encore, un nombre toujours croissant de destinations offraient des activités qui valaient la peine de dépenser du temps et de l'argent – plongée sous-marine, surf, pêche en haute-mer, jet-ski, parapente et beaucoup d'autres.

Le flux de touristes était devenu maintenant une marée et le vingt et unième siècle produisait déjà une nouvelle espèce de voyageurs. Il y a ceux qui sont prêts à dépenser une fortune pour un ticket pour s'embarquer dans l'espace. Quelques-uns ont réservé une cabine permanente sur un bateau de croisière et vivent maintenant à bord. Pour de telles personnes, voyager est devenu un mode de vie. Et pour des millions d'autres qui se présentent à l'enregistrement de leurs vols, qui montent dans un train ou qui se dirigent simplement vers l'autoroute la plus proche, libre ou à péage, il suffit de faire ce que beaucoup aiment par dessus tout – voyager.

DESTINATIONS
REISEZIELE
DESTINATIONS

FOR EVERY TRAVELLER there is a destination – a beach or a lake, a festival or an exhibition, a mountain or a monument. The fads and fashions come and go. Magazines, TV programmes, websites trumpet the delights of the latest hot-spot – where to go, what to see, what to wear, what to do, what to eat and drink. Yesterday it was Thailand, today it is Cuba, tomorrow…it could be anywhere. But always the old favourites remain, still making their siren call – Provence, New York, the Spanish *costas*, the Alps, the Nile, Amsterdam, Lake Como and a thousand more. Some have endured centuries of popularity which have almost worn them out. Visitors to Venice and Florence have to be rationed. The Acropolis and the Alhambra are under threat.

The traveller is spoilt for choice. Is it time to try something new, or to steal away for one more visit to a long lost love? Time to hack one's way through the Amazon jungle, or jet down to dear old Acapulco (the first resort to rely solely on the airplane as a means of access)? Time to see the sun rise over the Mongokian plains, or set over the rooftops of Paris? Time to blaze a trail across the tundra, or throw oneself once more into the colour and clamour of Mardi Gras?

For some, the destination is an entire continent. Tourists from America, Japan or Down-Under may have one chance only to visit Europe. They embark on a whirlwind tour that takes in the Sistine Chapel, the Brandenburg Gate, the Eiffel Tower, the Prado, Mozart's birthplace and Karl Marx's grave. They slake their thirsts and drive away their pangs of hunger in a Bavarian *beerhaus*, a pub in London, a *café* in Vienna. A dozen landscapes blur together as they glide along the motorways of Europe. If it's Tuesday, it must be Belgium. If it's flat, it must be Holland. If you can't get near it, it must be the *Mona Lisa*.

Change the continent and a similar superabundance of riches appears. What package tour of the United States could take in everything from Niagara Falls to the Grand Canyon, Bourbon Street to Harlem,

ABOVE

Victorian tourists take a break from the rigours of sightseeing among the ruins of the Temple of Jupiter, Athens, 1860. 'These edifices were all built of white Pentelic marble,' wrote Mark Twain, 'but have a pinkish stain upon them now. Where any part is broken, the fracture looks like fine loaf sugar.'

OPPOSITE

Tourists and guides in a frantic scramble up the rock slabs of an Egyptian pyramid, 1880. Such wear and tear on an historic monument would not be permitted today.

OBEN

Viktorianische Touristen erholen sich inmitten der Ruinen des Jupiter-Tempels in Athen von den Anstrengungen des Sightseeings (1860). „Die Gebäude wurden allesamt aus weißem Pentelic-Marmor erbaut", schrieb Mark Twain, „der inzwischen eine leichte Rosafärbung angenommen hat. Wo ein Stück heraus gebrochen ist, wirkt der Stein wie feiner Zucker."

RECHTE SEITE

Touristen und Reiseführer erklimmen mühevoll die Stein-stufen einer ägyptischen Pyramide (1880). Solch ein Umgang mit historischen Denkmälern wäre heutzutage undenkbar.

EN HAUT

Des touristes de l'ère victorienne se reposent parmi les ruines du Temple de Jupiter à Athènes après une journée de visite harassante, 1860. « Ces édifices furent tous construits en mar-bre blanc de Pentélique, mais présentent maintenant une tache rose. Là où une partie est cassée, la fracture ressemble à du pain de sucre », écrivait Mark Twain.

CI-CONTRE

Des touristes et des guides grimpent tant bien que mal sur les blocs de rocs d'une pyramide égyptienne, 1880. Une telle usure d'un monument historique ne serait pas permise de nos jours.

BELOW
Hula dancers on Honolulu's Waikiki Beach provide amateur moviemakers with the title credits for their show, 1953.

OPPOSITE
The proud proprietors of the *Bedouin Moon Restaurant*, Dahab, Sinai, Egypt display their menu.

UNTEN
Hula-Tänzerinnen am Strand von Waikiki in Honolulu liefern Amateurfilmern den Vorspann für ihr Werk (1953).

RECHTE SEITE
Die stolzen Besitzer des *Bedouin Moon Restaurant* in Dahab, Sinai, Ägypten, mit der Speisekarte.

EN BAS
Des danseuses de Hula sur la plage de Waikiki à Honolulu offrent à des cinéastes amateurs le générique de leur show, 1953.

CI-CONTRE
Les fiers propriétaires du restaurant *Bedouin Moon*, Dahab, Sinaï, Égypte posent devant la carte des menus.

Gracelands to the White House? How long a stay would be needed to do any sort of justice to the civilizations of Central and South America. How many days does India merit? How many years would China deserve?

Narrow the field of vision, and the problem remains. Fifty years ago skiers headed for the Alps. Now the *pistes* of the world stretch from Norway to New Zealand, from Austria to North America. Fifty years ago, surfers lay in wait for the Pacific rollers that battered on the shores of Hawaii and California. Today surfers from Brazil, Australia, Britain, France, Germany and the United States trawl the world for swells and tubes. Fifty years ago, the Mecca for golfers was Scotland. Now there are oases of well-manicured greens and gleaming fairways to be found in Dubai, the Caribbean, the Pacific Islands, and maybe one day in Mecca itself.

And fifty years ago, the great Walt Disney empire hit on the idea of creating an entirely new species of destination. On a plot of idle land in California, Disney built a make-believe mixture of the Wild West, King Arthur's Court and Never-Never Land. The huge success of Disneyland spawned the theme-park sequels of Disneyworld and EuroDisney. A whole new industry flattered Uncle Walt with imitations the world over – parks devoted to Space, War, comic strip heroes, Lego, the Arabian Nights, the Past, the Present and the Future.

Once upon a time, the traveller set out to meet the world. Now the world rushes to meet the traveller, creating time-share oases and hotel complexes in landscapes that were hitherto barren wildernesses. These tailor-made enclaves provide uniformity of four and five star comfort for the weary and sophisticated traveller in the Algarve, Goa, Borneo, Morocco, Bora Bora and points north, south, east and west. The architecture and the accommodation, the *cuisine* and the cocktails are standard. Familiarity breeds content.

CLOCKWISE FROM BOTTOM

In February 1964, two and a half years after it was built, the Berlin Wall still attracts coach-loads of visitors on the West Berlin side; Easter holidaymakers gather on the steps leading to the Sacré Coeur, Paris, 1979; American tourists rest their aching feet beside the Fountain of Trevi, Rome, 1955. The well-dressed gent with the silver topped cane is almost certainly a city guide.

IM UHRZEIGERSINN VON UNTEN

Im Februar 1964, zweieinhalb Jahre nach dem Bau, lockt die Berliner Mauer noch immer Busladungen neugieriger Besucher auf die Westberliner Seite; Osterurlauber rasten auf den Stufen der Kirche Sacré Coeur in Paris (1979); Amerikanische Touristen gönnen ihren schmerzenden Füßen am Brunnen von Trevi in Rom eine Pause (1955). Der gut gekleidete Herr mit dem Silber beschlagenen Gehstock ist mit ziemlicher Sicherheit ein Stadtführer.

DANS LE SENS DES AIGUILLES D'UNE MONTRE, A PARTIR DU BAS

En février 1964, deux ans et demi après sa construction, le Mur de Berlin attire encore des cars entiers de visiteurs du côté de Berlin Ouest. Des vacanciers à Pâques se rassemblent sur les marches menant au Sacré-Cœur, Paris, 1979. Des touristes américains font reposer leurs pieds endoloris près de la Fontaine de Trevi, Rome, 1955. Le personnage bien habillé avec une canne à l'extrémité d'argent est presque certainement un guide.

For those who prefer to see their jewels set in the gold of history, there are other places to stay, the Grand Hotels that offer a past and a pedigree. The man who began it all was César Ritz. At the age of twenty-seven, Ritz left his native Switzerland and travelled to Paris, looking for work at the time of the 1867 Exhibition. He got a job at the most fashionable hotel in the city – the *Splendide*. From there, he moved to Nice, as restaurant manager at the *Grand*. Ten years later he was manager of the *Grand National Hotel*, Lucerne. The rest of his career is a roll call of the greatest hotels in the world – the *Grand*, Monte Carlo; the *Savoy*, London; and finally, the *Ritz*, Paris. His name became synonymous with palatial comfort and faultless service, for he set the standard that others sought to emulate.

And so, a new chain of destinations was forged across the world, and a hundred years later a very precious few travellers pass through the portals of these temples of luxury – the *Crillon* in Paris, *Del Coronado* in San Diego, the *Hotel de Paris* in Monaco, *Claridges* in London, the *Waldorf-Astoria* in New York, the Hotel *Negresco* in Nice and the *Carlton* in Cannes. It is not enough to travel hopefully to such places. Here, one must arrive, and in style.

But there are plenty of other, more financially accessible places to go. There are campsites where we may pitch our tents or park our caravans in ordered array among forests of pines or by the water's edge on a stretch of golden sand. There are youth hostels perched halfway up mountains. There are holiday camps that offer everything from free entertainment to stolen romance. There are *chambres d'hotes* and farms that offer bed and breakfast, where visitors awake to the noise of a crowing cockerel and the smell of frying bacon sidling up the stairs. There are still unfinished barrack blocks on the Costa del Sol, palm thatched beach huts by the Indian Ocean, holiday chalets in a thousand resorts.

BOTTOM

A popular meeting place since the time of the Italian Renaissance. Tourists gather beside the Loggia dell' Orcagna (Loggia dei Lanzi) in the Piazza della Signoria, Florence in the 1930s. The ancient and beautiful paving slabs disappeared in the 1970s, a victim of renovation.

OPPOSITE

The most famous painting in the world – Leonardo da Vinci's *Mona Lisa* – gazes impassively back at early morning crowds gathering in the Louvre, Paris.

UNTEN

Ein beliebter Treffpunkt bereits seit der italienischen Renaissance. Touristen an der Loggia dell' Orcagna (Loggia dei Lanzi) an der Piazza della Signoria, Florenz (1930). Das altertümliche, wunderschöne Pflaster fiel der Renovierung in den siebziger Jahren zum Opfer.

RECHTE SEITE

Das berühmteste Gemälde der Welt – Leonardo da Vincis *Mona Lisa* blickt gelassen auf die frühmorgendliche Besucherschar im Louvre, Paris.

EN BAS

Une place de rencontre populaire depuis l'époque de la Renaissance italienne. Des touristes se rassemblent à côté de la Loggia dell'Orcagna (Loggia dei Lanzi) sur la Piazza della Signoria, Florence dans les années trente. Les anciens pavés magnifiques disparurent dans les années soixante-dix, victimes de la rénovation.

CI-CONTRE

Le tableau le plus célèbre du monde – *La Joconde* de Léonard de Vinci regarde, impassible, la foule qui afflue tôt le matin au Louvre, Paris.

For many travellers, however, overnight accommodation is merely a means to an end, a place of rest and recovery before another busy day at art galleries and museums (closed on Mondays), churches and cathedrals, shops and theatres. The earliest cheap excursion trips had been from city to countryside or seaside, but the exhibitions mounted in Paris, Vienna, Berlin, Chicago, St Louis and elsewhere in the late 19th century made such cities attractions in themselves. Today, one of the most popular holidays is the two or three day city-break.

In the wake of exhibitions came the new wave of festivals – opera at Bayreuth and Verona, film festivals in Cannes and Acapulco, jazz festivals in Newport and Barcelona, hundreds of literary festivals, children's festivals, dance festivals, and festivals to devoted to everything from beer to bull-running. Some have historical origins – the annual Palio in Siena dates back to the beginning of the 14th century. Others are the recent products of city publicity departments. All add to the world's wealth of attractions.

And so the lines of tourists and travellers form. Some are certain of their goals, of where they wish to go and what they wish to see. Others have a more open itinerary – what's on offer in Canada, Tunisia, the Gobi Desert, Copenhagen, the Carpathians, Lapland, Peru, the Mid West, the Near East, the Deep South, the far North?

For every traveller there is a destination.

BELOW
A lone traveller and a dusty station wagon take a break at the bottom of the Grand Canyon, Arizona.

OPPOSITE
Is it a dream? Is it a conceit? Is it a country? No, it's a theme park! A 1961 poster offers a glimspe of joy to come to WONDERLAND USA.

UNTEN
Ein einsamer Reisender und ein staubiger Kombi bei einer Pause auf dem Grund des Grand Canyon in Arizona.

RECHTE SEITE
Ist es ein Traum? Ist es ein Trugbild? Ist es ein Land? Nein! Es ist ein Erlebnispark! Das Plakat von 1961 macht Lust auf den Besuch des WONDERLAND USA.

EN BAS
Un voyageur solitaire et un station-wagon poussiéreux s'arrêtent en bas du Grand Canyon, Arizona.

CI-CONTRE
S'agit-il d'un rêve? D'une illusion? D'un pays? Non, c'est un parc à thème! Un poster de 1961 fait entrevoir le plaisir de visiter WONDERLAND USA.

BELOW
A lone traveller and a dusty station wagon take a break at the bottom of the Grand Canyon, Arizona.

UNTEN
Ein einsamer Reisender und ein staubiger Kombi bei einer Pause auf dem Grund des Grand Canyon in Arizona.

EN BAS
Un voyageur solitaire et un station-wagon poussiéreux s'arrêtent en bas du Grand Canyon, Arizona.

VISIT WONDERLAND USA

FÜR JEDEN REISENDEN existiert ein perfektes Reiseziel – ein Strand oder ein See, ein Festival oder eine Ausstellung, ein Berg oder ein Denkmal. Die Launen und Moden kommen und gehen. Zeitschriften, Fernsehprogramme und Webseiten trompeten die neuesten Hot-Spots hinaus – wohin man zu fahren, was man zu sehen, was zu tragen, was zu tun, was zu essen und zu trinken hat. Gestern war es Thailand, heute ist es Kuba und morgen... wo auch immer. Doch die alten Lieblingsplätze bleiben bestehen, locken weiterhin mit ihrem Sirenenruf – Provence, New York, die spanischen Küsten, die Alpen, der Nil, Amsterdam, der Comer See und Tausende mehr. Manche haben Jahrhunderte der Popularität überdauert und wurden dabei fast zerstört. Die Besucherzahl in Venedig und Florenz muss beschränkt werden, Akropolis und Alhambra drohen dasselbe Schicksal.

Der Reisende hat die Qual der Wahl. Ist es an der Zeit, etwas Neues auszuprobieren oder stiehlt man sich noch einmal fort zu einem letzten Besuch einer lang verlorenen Liebe? Ist es Zeit, sich einen Weg durch den Amazonasdschungel zu schlagen oder ins gute alte Acapulco zu jetten (dem ersten Ferienort, der nur mit dem Flugzeug zu erreichen ist)? Zeit, den Sonnenaufgang über den mongolischen Ebenen zu sehen oder den Sonnenuntergang über den Dächern von Paris? Zeit, einen Pfad durch die Tundra zu bahnen oder sich noch einmal in das Farbenmeer und den Lärm des *Mardi Gras* zu stürzen?

Für manche besteht das Reiseziel aus einem ganzen Kontinent. Touristen aus Amerika, Japan oder von *Down-under* haben vielleicht nur einmal Gelegenheit, Europa zu besuchen. Sie fegen über den Kontinent wie ein Wirbelwind und besuchen in kürzester Zeit die Sixtinische Kapelle, das Brandenburger Tor, den Eiffelturm, den Prado, Mozarts Geburtshaus und das Grab von Karl Marx. Sie stillen Hunger und Durst in einer bayerischen Brauereigaststätte, einem Pub in London, einem Café in Wien. Ein Dutzend Landschaften verschmelzen ineinander auf dem Weg über europäische Autobahnen. Wenn heute Dienstag ist, dann muss das hier Belgien sein. Wenn es flach ist, muss es Holland sein. Wenn du nicht in die Nähe kommst, ist es die *Mona Lisa*.

CLOCKWISE FROM OPPOSITE

The concrete cliffs of a high-rise hotel tower over Waikiki Beach, Honolulu, Hawaii – it's salutary to compare this picture with the 'Welcome' picture on page 88; A crowded beach on the shores of the Yellow Sea at Qingdao in Shandong Province, China; P&O Line's 'Take me away' poster; An aerial view of the sunbathing gridiron on Santa Monica beach, California.

AUF DER LINKEN SEITE BEGINNEND IM UHRZEIGERSINN

Die Betonklippen eines Hochhaus-Hotels am Waikiki Beach, Honolulu, Hawaii – ein Vergleich mit dem Willkommen-Foto auf Seite 88 ist aufschlussreich; Ein bevölkerter Strand am Gelben Meer bei Qingdao in der Provinz Shandong, China; „Take-me-away", Plakat der Reederei P&O; Ein Luftbild vom Sonnengrill Santa Monica Beach, Kalifornien.

DANS LE SENS DES AIGUILLES D'UNE MONTRE, A PARTIR DE LA PHOTO CI-CONTRE

Les falaises en béton d'une tour abritant un hôtel et surplombant la plage de Waikiki, Honolulu, Hawaii – il est réconfortant de comparer cette photo avec la photo de bienvenue de la page 88 ; une plage surpeuplée sur les côtes de la Mer Jaune à Qingdao dans la province de Shandong, Chine ; Poster « Emmène-moi !» de la P&O; Une vue aérienne du gril de bronzage de la plage de Santa Monica, Californie.

Ein Wechsel des Kontinents, und schon zeigt sich ein ähnlicher Überfluss an Reichtümern. Welcher Pauschalurlaub in den Vereinigten Staaten könnte all das beinhalten, von den Niagara Fällen bis zum Grand Canyon, von der Bourbon Street bis Harlem, von Graceland bis zum Weißen Haus? Wie lange müsste der Aufenthalt dauern, um den Kulturen Mittel- und Südamerikas einigermaßen gerecht zu werden? Wie viele Tage ist Indien wert? Wie viele Jahre hätte China verdient?

Auch wenn man den Blickwinkel begrenzt, bleibt ein Problem bestehen. Vor fünfzig Jahren fuhren die Skifahrer in die Alpen. Nun erstrecken sich die Pisten der Welt von Norwegen nach Neuseeland, von Österreich nach Nordamerika. Vor fünfzig Jahren warteten die Surfer im Pazifik vor Hawaii und Kalifornien auf „die Welle". Heute reisen Surfer aus Brasilien, Australien, England, Frankreich, Deutschland und den Vereinigten Staaten auf der Suche nach Wellen und Röhren um die Welt. Vor fünfzig Jahren lag das Mekka der Golfer in Schottland. Heute finden sich Oasen mit sorgfältig gepflegten Greens und schimmernden Fairways in Dubai, in der Karibik, auf den Pazifischen Inseln und vielleicht eines Tages selbst in Mekka.

Ebenfalls vor fünfzig Jahren baute das große Walt-Disney-Imperium auf die Idee, eine völlig neue Art von Reisezielen zu entwickeln. Auf einem brachliegenden Grundstück in Kalifornien errichtete Disney eine Phantasiewelt in einer Mischung aus Wild West, König Arthurs Hof und Traumgestaden. Der riesige Erfolg von Disneyland brachte die Themenpark-Ableger Disneyworld und EuroDisney hervor. Eine komplett neue Industrie schmeichelte Onkel Walt durch Imitationen seiner Parks auf der ganzen Welt – zu Themen wie Weltraum, Krieg, Comic-Helden, Lego, Arabische Nacht, Vergangenheit, Gegenwart und Zukunft.

Es war einmal, da zog der Reisende aus in die Welt. Heute kommt die Welt zum Reisenden in Form von Timeshare-Oasen und Hotelanlagen in Gegenden, wo es bisher nur karge Wildnis gab. Diese maßgeschnei-

derten Enklaven bieten die Uniformität von 4- und 5-Sterne-Komfort für den müde gewordenen und kultivierten Reisenden an der Algarve, auf Goa, Borneo, in Marokko, auf Bora Bora und überall im Norden, Süden, Osten oder Westen. Architektur und Unterkunft, Küche und Cocktails sind Standard, Vertrautheit erzeugt Zufriedenheit.

Jenen, die es vorziehen, ihre Juwelen im goldenen Glanz der Geschichte schimmern zu sehen, bieten sich andere Orte – die Grandhotels mit Vergangenheit und Stammbaum. Der Mann, mit dem alles begann, war César Ritz. Im Alter von 27 Jahren verließ Ritz seine Heimat, die Schweiz, und reiste nach Paris, um dort während der Weltausstellung 1867 Arbeit zu suchen. Er bekam einen Job im modernsten Hotel der Stadt – dem *Splendide*. Von hier aus ging er als Restaurantmanager nach Nizza ins *Grand Hôtel*. Zehn Jahre später war er Manager des *Grand National Hotel* in Luzern. Der Rest seiner Karriere gleicht einer Aufzählung der größten Hotels der Welt – das *Grand Hôtel* in Monte Carlo, das *Savoy* in London und schließlich das *Ritz* in Paris. Sein Name wurde zum Synonym für feudalen Komfort und tadellosen Service. Er setzte den Standard, dem andere nach zu eifern suchten.

So wurde eine neue Kette von Reisezielen rund um die Welt geschmiedet. Einhundert Jahre später traten einige wenige hochverehrte Reisende durch die Portale dieser Luxustempel – des *Crillon* in Paris, des *Del Coronado* in San Diego, *des Hôtel de Paris* in Monaco, des *Claridges* in London, des *Waldorf-Astoria* in New York, des *Negresco* in Nizza und des *Carlton* in Cannes. Es genügt nicht, hoffnungsfroh an solche Orte zu reisen. Hier muss man ankommen, und zwar mit Stil.

Doch es gibt viele andere, finanziell eher erreichbare Orte. Es gibt Campingplätze, auf denen wir unsere Zelte und Wohnwagen in geordneten Reihen in Pinienwäldern oder an einem goldenen Sandstrand aufstellen können. Es gibt Jugendherbergen, die an Berghängen thronen. Es gibt Clubanlagen, die von kostenloser Unterhaltung bis zur heimlichen Romanze alles bieten. Es gibt Gästezimmer und Bauernhöfe mit Übernachtung und Frühstück, wo die Besucher beim Schrei des Hahns mit dem Duft von gebratenem Speck in der Nase erwachen. Es gibt die noch immer unfertigen Hotelkasernen an der Costa del Sol, palmengedeckte Strandhütten am Indischen Ozean und Ferienhäuser in Tausenden von Urlaubsorten.

CLOCKWISE FROM OPPOSITE

The *Elephant Hotel*, Atlantic City, New Jersey, 1907; The giant bear icon outside a Wyoming hotel in the USA; Tourist cabins on the highway near Bardstown, Kentucky, 1940; The retired *RMS Queen Mary* – floating museum, hotel and shopping centre at Long Beach, California, 1975; *Glitter Gulch*, Las Vegas, Nevada; Veldon Simpson's *Luxor Hotel*, Las Vegas, 1993.

IM UHRZEIGERSINN VON LINKS

The Elephant Hotel, Atlantic City, New Jersey (1907); Riesiger Bär, Wahrzeichen eines Hotels in Wyoming, USA; Hütten für Touristen am Highway bei Bardstown, Kentucky (1940); Die ausgediente *RMS Queen Mary* – ein schwimmendes Museum, Hotel und Einkaufszentrum in Long Beach, Kalifornien (1975); *Glitter Gulch*, Las Vegas, Nevada; Veldon Simpsons *Hotel Luxor*, Las Vegas (1993); .

DANS LE SENS DES AIGUILLES D'UNE MONTRE, A PARTIR DE LA GAUCHE

L' Elephant Hotel, Atlantic City, New Jersey, 1907; Représentation d'un ours géant à l'extérieur d'un hôtel du Wyoming aux Etats-Unis; Des tentes pour touristes sur l'autoroute près de Bardstown, Kentucky, 1940; Le *RMS Queen Mary* à la retraite – musée flottant, hôtel et centre commercial à Long Beach, Californie, 1975; Le *Glitter Gulch*, Las Vegas, Nevada; L'hôtel *Luxor* de Veldon Simpson, Las Vegas, 1993.

CLOCKWISE FROM OPPOSITE
Lucius Beebe forsakes his private railcar for the splendour of
the *Garden Court* of the *Palace Hotel*, San Francisco; One of
the biggest luxury hotels in the world – the 750 bedroom
Hotel Coronado, San Diego, USA; One of the most beautifully
sited hotels in the world – the *Carlton Hotel*, Cannes, France;
In its heyday, the biggest hotel in the world – the *Astor*, New
York City, 1912.

LINKE SEITE BEGINNEND IM UHRZEIGERSINN
Lucius Beebe tauscht seinen privaten Eisenbahnwaggon
gegen die Pracht des *Garden Court* im *Palace Hotel*, San
Francisco, ein; Eines der größten Luxushotels der Welt – das
Hotel Coronado mit 750 Zimmern, San Diego, USA; Eines der
schönst gelegenen Hotels der Welt – das *Carlton*, Cannes,
Frankreich; Die Blütezeit des größten Hotels der Welt – das
Astor, New York City (1912).

DANS LE SENS DES AIGUILLES D'UNE MONTRE, A PARTIR
DE LA PHOTO CI-CONTRE
Lucius Beebe quitte son wagon privé pour la splendeur du
Garden Court du *Palace Hotel*, San Francisco. Un des plus
grands hôtels de luxe du monde – l'hôtel *Coronado* com-
prenant 750 chambres, San Diego, USA. Un des hôtels les
mieux situés du monde – l'hôtel *Carlton*, Cannes, France. À
son âge d'or, le plus grand hôtel du monde – L'hôtel *Astor*,
New York City, 1912.

Für viele Reisende ist die Unterkunft jedoch lediglich ein Mittel zum Zweck, ein Ort der Ruhe und Erholung vor einem neuen geschäftigen Tag in Kunstgalerien und Museen (montags geschlossen), Kirchen und Kathedralen, Läden und Theatern. Die ersten preiswerten Ausflüge waren die von der Stadt aufs Land oder ans Meer, doch die in Paris, Wien, Berlin, Chicago, St. Louis und anderswo im späten 19. Jahrhundert organisierten Ausstellungen ließen die Städte selbst zu Sehenswürdigkeiten werden. Heute gehören zwei- oder dreitägige Städtereisen zu den beliebtesten Urlaubsformen.

Den Ausstellungen folgte die neue Welle der Festivals – Oper in Bayreuth und Verona, Filmfestivals in Cannes und Acapulco, Jazzfestivals in Newport und Barcelona, Hunderte von Literaturfestivals, Kinderfestivals, Tanzfestivals und Festivals, die allem möglichen, vom Bier bis hin zum Bullenrennen, gewidmet waren. Einige sind historischen Ursprungs – der alljährliche *Palio* in Siena geht beispielsweise auf den Anfang des 14. Jahrhunderts zurück. Andere sind die neuesten Produkte städtischer Ämter für Öffentlichkeitsarbeit. Alle vergrößern den Reichtum der Welt an Sehenswürdigkeiten.

So formieren sich die Reihen der Touristen und Reisenden. Einige sind sich ihrer Ziele sicher, wissen, wohin sie gehen und was sie sehen möchten. Andere lassen ihre Reiseroute eher offen – was haben Kanada, Tunesien, die Wüste Gobi, Kopenhagen, die Karpaten, Lappland, Peru, der Mittlere Westen, der Nahe Osten, tiefe Süden oder der ferne Norden zu bieten?

Für jeden Reisenden existiert ein perfektes Reiseziel.

ABOVE

Tents and caravans snuggle together at a campsite near Kiel, Western Germany, 1972.

OPPOSITE

Fifty thousand cross country runners camp at Västerhaninge, near Stockholm.

OBEN

Zelte und Wohnwagen auf einem Campingplatz bei Kiel, (1972).

RECHTE SEITE

Fünfzigtausend Langstreckenläufer campieren in Vasterhaninge bei Stockholm.

EN-HAUT

Des tentes et des caravanes blotties l'une contre l'autre dans un camping près de Kiel, 1972.

CI-CONTRE

Cinquante mille coureurs de cross country campent à Vasterhaninge près de Stockholm.

TOUT VOYAGEUR a une destination – une plage ou un lac, un festival ou une exposition, une montagne ou un monument. Les modes et les engouements vont et viennent. Les magazines, les programmes TV, les sites internet vantent les attraits du dernier point chaud de la planète – où aller, que voir, comment se vêtir, que faire, que boire et manger. Hier c'était la Thaïlande, aujourd'hui c'est Cuba, demain … cela pourrait être n'importe où. Toutefois les destinations favorites d'autrefois continuent d'attirer les touristes et de les séduire comme par un chant de sirènes – la Provence, New York, les *costas* espagnoles, les Alpes, le Nil, Amsterdam, le Lac de Côme et des milliers d'autres. Certains endroits ont tellement supporté des siècles de popularité qu'ils en sont presque altérés. Le nombre de visiteurs à Venise et à Florence doit être limité. L'Acropole et l'Alhambra sont menacés.

Le voyageur a l'embarras du choix. S'agit-il d'essayer une destination nouvelle ou de retourner une fois de plus vers des amours perdus ? S'agit-il de se frayer un chemin à travers la forêt amazonienne ou bien de s'embarquer sur un avion à destination de cette chère Acapulco (le premier lieu de vacance accessible seulement par avion) ? S'agit-il de voir le lever du soleil sur les plaines mongoliennes ou d'admirer les toits de Paris ? S'agit-il de se frayer un chemin à travers la toundra ou de se perdre dans les couleurs et les clameurs du Mardi gras ?

Pour certains, la destination est un continent entier. Les touristes d'Amérique, du Japon ou d'Australie et de Nouvelle-Zélande peuvent bien avoir une seule chance de visiter l'Europe. Ils s'embarquent pour un tour éclair qui les emmène à la Chapelle Sixtine, à la Porte de Brandebourg, à la Tour Eiffel, au Prado, au lieu de naissance de Mozart et sur la tombe de Karl Marx. Ils étanchent leur soif et soulagent les tiraillements d'estomac provoqués par la faim dans une brasserie bavaroise, dans un pub à Londres ou un café à Vienne. Une dizaine de paysages se confondent alors qu'ils roulent sur les autoroutes d'Europe. Si c'est mardi, il faut aller en Belgique. Si ce doit être plat, il faut aller aux Pays-Bas. Si on ne peut pas s'en approcher, ce doit être la Joconde.

Changeons de continent et une surabondance similaire de diversités apparaît. Quel voyage organisé aux États-Unis vous emmènerait partout des Chutes du Niagara au Grand Canyon, de Bourbon Street à Harlem, de Gracelands à la Maison Blanche ? Combien de temps devrait durer le séjour pour faire un tant soit peu honneur aux civilisations d'Amérique Centrale et d'Amérique du Sud ? Combien de jours mérite l'Inde ? Combien d'années mériterait la Chine ?

Si l'on rétrécit son champ de vision, le problème demeure. Il y a cinquante ans, les skieurs se rendaient dans les Alpes. Maintenant les pistes dans le monde se trouvent de la Norvège à la Nouvelle-Zélande, de l'Autriche à l'Amérique du Nord. Il y a cinquante ans, les surfeurs s'allongeaient en attendant les vagues du Pacifique qui déferlaient sur les côtes d'Hawaii et de Californie. Aujourd'hui les surfeurs du Brésil, d'Australie, de Grande-Bretagne, de France, d'Allemagne et des États-Unis parcourent le monde en quête de vagues déferlantes et de rouleaux. Il y a cinquante ans, la Mecque du golf était l'Écosse. Aujourd'hui, on trouve des oasis de greens impeccables et des fairways étincelants à Dubai, dans les Caraïbes, les îles du Pacifique et peut-être un jour même à la Mecque.

ABOVE
Friends gather by the poolside at a desert house in Palm Springs, California, USA.

OPPOSITE
Hot sand, warm wicker and sunny smiles on a well-appointed beach.

OBEN
Freunde versammeln sich am Pool eines Hauses in der Wüste von Palm Springs, Kalifornien, USA.

LINKE SEITE
Heißer Sand, warmer Korb und sonnige Mienen an einem gut besuchten Strand.

EN HAUT
Des amis se rassemblent au bord de la piscine d'une maison dans le désert à Palm Springs, Californie, USA.

CI-CONTRE
Le sable chaud, des fauteuils en rotin et des sourires chaleureux sur une plage très fréquentée.

Et il y a cinquante ans, le grand empire de Walt Disney eut l'idée de créer un genre tout nouveau de destination. Sur un vaste terrain vague en Californie, Disney construisit un mélange de fantaisie entre le Far West, la cour du Roi Arthur et un pays imaginaire. Le succès considérable de Disneyland entraîna la création d'autres parcs à thèmes Disneyworld et EuroDisney. Une industrie entièrement nouvelle flatta l'oncle Walt avec des imitations partout dans le monde – des parcs consacrés à l'espace, à la guerre, à des héros de bandes dessinées, aux Lego, aux Mille et Une Nuits, au passé, au présent et au futur.

Autrefois, le voyageur partait à la découverte du monde. Maintenant, c'est le monde qui s'élance à la rencontre du voyageur en créant des oasis multi-propriété et des complexes hôteliers dans des paysages qui étaient jusqu'ici des régions reculées et arides. Ces enclaves créées sur mesure offrent aux voyageurs épuisés et sophistiqués un confort uniforme à quatre ou cinq étoiles dans l'Algarve, à Goa, à Bornéo, au Maroc, à Bora-Bora et aux quatre points cardinaux. L'architecture et l'ameublement, la cuisine et les cocktails sont standards. Ce qui est familier satisfait.

Ceux qui préfèrent le luxe allié à la tradition choisiront de séjourner dans les Grands Hôtels qui offrent à la fois un passé et une renommée. L'homme qui commença tout cela s'appelait César Ritz. À l'âge de vingt-sept ans, Ritz quitta sa Suisse natale et voyagea à Paris à la recherche d'un emploi au moment de l'exposition de 1867.

Il obtint un poste dans l'hôtel le plus luxueux de la ville – le *Splendide*. De là, il se rendit à Nice, comme responsable des restaurants du *Grand Hôtel*. Dix ans plus tard, il était le directeur du *Grand National Hotel* de Lucerne. Le reste de sa carrière, il répond à l'appel des plus prestigieux hôtels du monde – le *Grand Hôtel* de Monte-Carlo, le *Savoy* de Londres et finalement le *Ritz* de Paris. Son nom devint synonyme de confort digne de palace et de service irréprochable étant donné qu'il fixait des standards que tous les autres tentaient d'imiter.

C'est ainsi qu'une nouvelle chaîne de destinations s'était forgée à travers le monde et que cent ans plus tard quelques voyageurs fortunés passent les portes de ces temples du luxe – le *Crillon* à Paris, le *Del Coronado* à San Diego, l'*Hôtel de Paris* à Monaco, le *Claridges* à Londres, le *Waldorf-Astoria* à New York, le *Negresco* à Nice et le *Carlton* à Cannes. Il ne suffit pas d'espérer voyager dans de tels endroits. Ici, il s'agit d'arriver, et en grande pompe.

Toutefois, il y a de nombreux endroits plus abordables où se rendre. Il y a des campings où l'on peut planter sa tente ou garer sa caravane dans des allées ordonnées dans des forêts de pins ou au bord de l'eau sur une plage de sable fin. Il y a des auberges de jeunesse perchées dans la montagne. Il y a des villages de vacances qui offrent aussi bien des activités gratuites que des romances volées. Il y a des chambres d'hôtes

CLOCKWISE FROM OPPOSITE

The swinging scene at Rimini beach on the Italian Adriatic coast, 1956; Fun and fright on a water-toboggan at Cypress Gardens, Florida, USA, 28th August 1968; Playing the poolside machines at the *Sands Hotel*, Las Vegas, May 1965 – note the approaching waitress; Carmen Alvarez and Frank 'Brandy' Brandstetter enjoy wet backgammon in an Acapulco pool, January 1978.

IM UHRZEIGERSINN VON LINKS

Fröhliche Schaukelszene am Strand von Rimini an der italienischen Adria (1956); Spaß und Schrecken auf einem Wasserschlitten in Cypress Gardens, Florida, USA (28. August 1968); Spiel an den Einarmigen Banditen am Pool des *Sands Hotel*, Las Vegas (Mai 1965) – achten Sie auf die sich nähernde Kellnerin; Carmen Alvarez und Frank „Brandy" Brandstetter beim Backgammon in einem Swimmingpool in Acapulco (Januar 1978).

DANS LE SENS DES AIGUILLES D'UNE MONTRE, A PARTIR DE LA GAUCHE

Balancement endiablé sur la plage de Rimini sur la Côte Adriatique en Italie, 1956. Frayeur et amusement sur un toboggan à eau à Cypress Gardens, Floride, USA, 28 août 1968. Jeu aux machines à sous de la piscine du *Sands Hotel* à Las Vegas, mai 1965 – à noter la serveuse qui s'approche. Carmen Alvarez et Frank Brandstetter surnommé « Brandy » jouent au backgammon dans une piscine d'Acapulco, janvier 1978.

RIGHT

Didi Fenton holes her putt on the St Moritz course,
February 1983.

OPPOSITE

An all bunker course of sand at the *Mena House Golf Club*,
in the shadow of the Great Pyramid of Giza, Egypt,
28th March 1938.

RECHTS

Didi Fenton locht auf dem Golfplatz von St. Moritz ein
(Februar 1983).

LINKE SEITE

Einen Course komplett aus Sandbunkern bietet der *Mena
House Golf Club* im Schatten der Pyramiden von Giseh,
Ägypten (28. März 1938).

A DROITE

Didi Fenton fait un trou sur le terrain de golf de Saint-Moritz,
février 1983.

CI-CONTRE

Un terrain de golf constitué de tout un bunker de sable au
club de golf de *Mena House*, à l'ombre de la grande pyramide
de Gizeh en Égypte, 28 mars 1938.

CLOCKWISE FROM OPPOSITE

Straining the eyes but resting the limbs – a skiing party gazes down at the slopes, 1955; Skiers queue for their turn on the piste at Kitzbuhel, Austria, 12th December 1938; A 1926 poster depicting winter sports at Mont-Revard, France.

AUF DER LINKEN SEITE BEGINNEND IM UHRZEIGERSINN

Anstrengung für die Augen, doch Entspannung für die Glieder – eine Gruppe Skifahrer blickt die Piste hinab (1955); Skifahrer sammeln sich zur Abfahrt in Kitzbühel, Österreich (12. Dezember 1938); Ein Plakat aus dem Jahr 1926 wirbt für den Wintersport am Mont-Revard in Frankreich.

DANS LE SENS DES AIGUILLES D'UNE MONTRE, A PARTIR DE LA PHOTO CI-CONTRE

Effort pour les yeux, mais repos pour les membres – un groupe de skieurs regardent en bas des pistes, 1955. Les skieurs font la file pour avoir leur tour sur les pistes de Kitzbuhel, Autriche, 12 décembre 1938. Un poster de 1926 fait la promotion des sports d'hiver à Mont-Revard en France.

et des fermes qui offrent la possibilité du *bed & breakfast*, où les visiteurs sont réveillés par le chant du coq et par l'odeur alléchante du lard fumé. Il y a les immeubles toujours inachevés de la Costa del Sol, les bungalows aux toits de paille près de l'Océan Indien et des chalets de vacance dans des milliers de lieux touristiques.

Toutefois, le logement ne représente pour beaucoup de voyageurs qu'un moyen pour arriver à ses fins, un endroit pour se reposer et récupérer des forces avant une autre journée bien remplie de visites de galeries d'art et de musées (fermés le lundi), d'églises et de cathédrales, de magasins et de théâtre. Autrefois, les excursions à bon marché avaient lieu de la ville à la campagne ou à la mer, mais les grandes expositions de la fin du 19ème siècle montaient vers Paris, Vienne, Berlin, Chicago, St. Louis et ailleurs rendant ces villes des attractions en soi. Aujourd'hui, les séjours de deux ou trois jours dans les grandes villes sont devenues parmi les plus populaires.

Après la vague des grandes expositions vint la vague des festivals – le festival de l'opéra à Bayreuth et à Vérone, le festival du film à Cannes et à Acapulco, le festival du jazz à Newport et à Barcelone, des centaines de festival de la littérature, de festivals pour enfants, de festivals de danse et de festivals dédiés aussi bien à la bière qu'à la tauromachie. Certains ont des origines historiques – le *Palio* annuel de Sienne remonte au début du 14ème siècle. D'autres sont des créations récentes des syndicats d'initiative des villes. Tous contribuent à la variété des attractions dans le monde.

C'est ainsi que des files de touristes et de voyageurs se forment. Certains sont certains de leurs destinations et d'où ils veulent aller exactement et de ce qu'ils veulent visiter. D'autres ont un itinéraire plus flexible – Que peut on voir actuellement au Canada, en Tunisie, dans le désert de Gobi, à Copenhague, dans les Carpates, en Laponie, au Pérou, dans le Middle West, au Proche-Orient, dans le grand Sud et au pôle Nord ?

Tout voyageur a une destination.

TRAVEL ACCESSORIES
REISEZUBEHÖR
ACCESSOIRES DE VOYAGE

IN FEBRUARY 1933, eighteen-year-old Patrick Leigh Fermor set out to walk from Rotterdam to Constantinople. His kit consisted of an old Army greatcoat, jersey, flannel shirt, trousers, puttees, thick socks and nailed boots. His luxury items were a sleeping bag, notebooks and pencils, a walking stick and *The Oxford Book of English Verse* – all of which he lost within a few weeks. The thousand mile journey took him three years to complete.

Sooner or later, regular travellers identify an object that they must take with them wherever they go – a travelling companion. It may be a special pillow or a cushion, a Swiss Army knife or a pair of binoculars, a bum-bag or a rucksack. There are those who cannot bear to take a single step without map or guidebook. The threat of mosquitoes or melanoma compels many more to pack insect repellent and sun-cream (the modern equivalent of the Victorian parasol). The prudent take a First Aid kit. The adventurous make sure they have compass or global navigation aid, for there are plenty of places in the world where it is possible to get hopelessly lost.

Fermor didn't bother with any of this. He took a little money and arranged that five pounds should be available each month at *poste restante* addresses spread along his route. Had he been able to afford the initial outlay, he could have used Travellers' Cheques, for they had long been in existence. In 1873, Thomas Cook issued 'circular notes', a forerunner of the cheques pioneered by *American Express* in 1891. Today the problem of day-to-day finances while on the move has been solved by just forty square centimetres of plastic. The credit card is perhaps the greatest travelling aid of all time, working its magic to provide tickets, meals, clothes, shelter, souvenirs and a deceptively endless supply of local currency. The pleasure and relief it supplies come first. The bill comes later.

Fermor was that rare individual, the lone traveller. Not for him the assistance of agent, dragoman or rep. He spurned the services of the vast empire created nearly a century earlier by the enterprise of one man. On 5th July 1841, Thomas Cook organised the first publicly advertised excursion by train. The outing was from

CLOCKWISE FROM ABOVE

A would-be traveller collects leaflets from the publicity van of the *London Midland and Scottish Railway*, 28th June 1930; The first edition of *Baedeker's Guide*, 1830; The cover of the *Rough Guide to Guatemala*, the first to be published in the series; Maps of the 1850s, showing overland routes to India; A Michelin map of the British Isles from 1914; Seeking to seduce the travelling public.

IM UHRZEIGERSINN VON OBEN

Eine Möchtegern-Reisende sammelt Reklamezettel am Werbewagen der *London Midland and Scottish Railway* (28. Juni 1930); Die erste Ausgabe des Baedeker-Reiseführers von 1830; Das Titelbild des *Rough Guide to Guatemala*, des ersten seiner Serie; Landkarten aus den fünfziger Jahren des 19. Jahrhunderts mit Überlandrouten nach Indien; Eine Michelin-Karte der Britischen Inseln von 1914; Der Versuch, das reisende Publikum zu verführen.

DANS LE SENS DES AIGUILLES D'UNE MONTRE, A PARTIR DU HAUT

Un voyageur potentiel récolte des dépliants d'une camionnette publicitaire de la *London Midland and Scottish Railway*, 28 juin 1930. La première édition du Guide de Baedeker, 1830. Couverture du *Rough Guide to Guatemala*, le premier de la série à avoir été publié. Cartes de 1850 indiquant les routes par voie de terre vers l'Inde. Carte Michelin des Îles Britanniques de 1914. Tentative de séduction des touristes.

Leicester to a temperance rally in Loughborough, and the cost was one shilling (5p) per head. It was an immediate success. Cook went on to arrange trips to the seaside, to Paris and to the battlefield of Waterloo. In 1851, Cook transported 165,000 visitors to the Great Exhibition in London's Hyde Park. By the 1870s, he was running trips to almost every country in the world, had links with over 500 hotels, and sold tickets to 344,739 out of 369,495 railways operating in the world. 'There are spots on the sun BUT not a spot on earth that you cannot visit with the aid of Cook's Tickets,' boasted one of his advertisements. Cook was the King of Travel. 'Unprotected females confide in him,' wrote a contemporary. 'Hypochondriacs tell him of their complaints, foolish travellers look to him to redeem their errors…'

Cook's skill and success in organising travel for the masses provoked a string of competitors. Carl Stangen of Berlin arranged his first Round-the-World tour in 1878. It attracted only seven clients, but Stangen persevered. By 1889, there were plenty of takers for similar tours that took eight months to complete and cost over 11,000 marks. In 1893, Sir Henry Lunn, founder of the travel firm that still bears his name, organised his first excursion, a trip to Switzerland, for Lunn was himself a keen mountaineer. Today there is a travel bureau in every city in the world.

Travellers became better protected and better informed. A whole new industry sprang up to cater for their requirements. Fortnums of London sold 100 kilos of cocoa powder to Sir Edward Parry when he set out in 1819 to search for the Northwest Passage. In the early 1830s, William James Adams opened a shop in Fleet Street where he sold all that a traveller might need, from guidebooks and passports to insect powder. A generation later, a group of army and navy officers formed a co-operative that catered for servicemen and their families, with special emphasis on travelling supplies. It was said that the intending traveller could purchase anything from a needle to an elephant at the new *Army and Navy Stores*.

One of the earliest guidebooks was Thomas Martyn's *Guide to France* of 1787, complete with a scale of up to four exclamation marks (similar to the Michelin rosettes) to denote the importance of individual paintings in galleries and museums. The first professional guidebook writer was Mariana Stokes, who published her *Letters from Italy* in 1820. But the most famous series of guides are those of Carl Baedeker. In 1829, Baedeker bought a failing publishing house whose list included a *Guidebook to Koblenz*. From this humble beginning, he went on to produce guidebooks that covered the whole of Europe, with the aim of providing enough print-

Your Easter Holiday will last you twice as long if you
Take a Kodak with you.

The No. 2
FOLDING POCKET KODAK
Daylight Loading and Changing.

For Pictures 3½ x 3½.   Price £3 3s.

THE NEW MODEL IS THE BEST VALUE IN CAMERAS YET OFFERED.

Fitted with our splendid New Automatic Focussing Device. Fixed-focus simplicity with
adjustable-focus range and rapidity.

*Write for Prospectus of the Kodak 1905 Competition. £400 IN PRIZES for
Pictures taken with a Kodak on Kodak N.C. Film.*

May be obtained from all Dealers, or from

KODAK, LTD.   57-61, Clerkenwell Road
LONDON, E.C.

BRANCHES: 96, Bold Street, LIVERPOOL; 72-74, Buchanan Street, GLASGOW;
59, Brompton Road, S.W.; 60, Cheapside, E.C.; 115, Oxford Street, W.;
171-173, Regent Street, W.; and 40, Strand, LONDON, W.C.

ernemann
cameras

gelten als unübertrefflich. Unser stetes Be-
mühen, auch die bewährtesten Modelle weiter
zu verbessern und zu vervollkommnen,
rechtfertigt dieses Vertrauen und macht jeden
Käufer zum überzeugten Freund unseres Er-
zeugnisses. Bezug durch alle Photohandlungen.
Preisliste kostenfrei.

ERNEMANN-WERKE A-G. DRESDEN 114
Photo-Kino-Werke   Optische Anstalt.

CLOCKWISE FROM BOTTOM LEFT

An advertisement from *Simplicissimus* for the German-made Ernemann cameras of 1919; A 1905 advertisement for the *No 2 Kodak Folding Pocket Camera*, boasting that 'your Easter Holiday will last twice as long if you take a Kodak with you…'; Early Kodak 'Box' cameras – a *Hawkeye Brownie No 2* (left) and a *Brownie 6-20* with its carrying case; A French passport issued not long after the Franco-Prussian War of 1870-1871 – note that the issuing authority is now the *République Francaise*, following the collapse of the Empire; The British joint passport issued to Mr and Mrs D F Landor in 1921; A ticket to travel by *Peninsular and Oriental Steam Navigation Company* from Calcutta (India) to Southampton (England) at a cost of 400 rupees, leaving on 8th April 1847.

IM UHRZEIGERSINN VON LINKS UNTEN

Eine Anzeige im *Simplicissimus* für die in Deutschland hergestellte Kamera der Firma Ernemann (1919); In der 1905 erschienenen Anzeige für die *Kodak Folding Pocket Kamera Nr. 2* wird behauptet: „Ihr Osterurlaub dauert zweimal so lange, wenn Sie eine Kodak mit nehmen…"; Frühe Kodak Kastenkamera – eine *Hawkeye Brownie No. 2* (links) und eine *Brownie 6-20* mit Tasche; Ein französischer Pass, ausgestellt kurz nach dem deutsch-französischen Krieg von 1870/71 – man kann erkennen, dass die ausstellende Autorität nach dem Zusammenbruch des Reiches, nun die *République Francaise* ist; Der gemeinsame Pass von Mr. und Mrs. D.F. Landor von 1921; Ein Ticket der *Peninsular and Oriental Steam Navigation Company* für die Reise von Kalkutta (Indien) nach Southampton (England) zum Preis von 400 Rupien mit Abfahrtsdatum vom 8. April 1847.

DANS LE SENS DES AIGUILLES D'UNE MONTRE, A PARTIR DU BAS GAUCHE

Une publicité de 1919 parue dans *Simplicissimus* pour des appareils-photo Ernemann fabriqués en Allemagne. Publicité de 1905 pour l'appareil-photo de poche *Kodak No 2* utilisant le slogan suivant : « Vos vacances de Pâques dureront deux fois plus longtemps si vous emportez un Kodak avec vous… ». Les premiers appareils-photo du modèle le plus rudimentaire – un *Brownie No 2* de l'Iowa (à gauche) et un *Brownie 6-20* avec sa pochette. Passeport français délivré peu de temps après la guerre franco-prussienne de 1870-1871 – à noter que l'autorité de délivrance est maintenant la République Française à la suite de l'effondrement de l'Empire. Passeport commun britannique délivré à M. et Mme D F Landor en 1921. Billet de transport pour voyager avec la *Peninsular and Oriental Steam Navigation Company* de Calcutta (Inde) jusqu'à Southampton (Angleterre) pour le prix de 400 roupies, départ le 8 avril 1847.

ed information for travellers to be able to dispense with the services of paid guides. Today's *Michelin Guides*, *Rough Guides*, *Fodor's Guides* and *Lonely Planet Guides* are following in Baedeker's printed footsteps.

In the wake of guidebooks came timetables and maps. The British Ordnance Survey large scale maps first appeared in 1805. Their initial aim was to help plan England's coastal defences against invasion by Napoleon Bonaparte, but they quickly became popular with travellers and holiday-makers. The brothers Michelin – always keen to encourage the use of the motor car, and hence the sale of their tyres – published maps covering most of Europe, and Rand McNally did the same for Canada, the United States and Mexico.

In 1873, when he was plotting *Around the World in Eighty Days*, Jules Verne used Bradshaw's Rail Guide to work out the shortest possible time in which a circumnavigation of the globe was possible. George Bradshaw was an engraver and printer who published the first Railway Timetable to bear his name in 1839, and his first Continental Railway Guide in 1847 – twenty-six years before Cook's first Continental Timetable appeared. It was a monumental task, for rail companies changed their schedules almost every month, with little notice, but Bradshaw and his assistants stuck to their work and played a large part in bringing order to the European rail network.

Slowly but steadily, there evolved solutions for every travel problem. The jumbo jet dramatically reduced the cost of inter-continental travel. Drugs and medicines became available to combat the world's deadlier diseases. Mosquito nets brought freedom from the misery of many a tropical night. Engineers and chemists joined forces to make sea travel more comfortable – the former with the development of stabilisers on ships, the latter with cures for seasickness. Mothersill's Seasick Remedy first appeared in the 1920s, followed later by the hopefully named 'Kwells', but the real breakthrough came with the invention of a synthetic anti-histamine called Dramamine in the 1940s. New fabrics and alloys provided the backpacker with tents that weighted less than a kilo. Luggage for the less rugged became lighter but sturdier. Modern systems of communication made it possible to stay in touch or call for help from one side of the world to the other.

Today the economy of many countries relies on tourism, and whole areas of land and coast have been dedicated to the needs of the traveller. There are those who fear overkill – too many going too far too often. But the glory and glamour of taking off remains.

IM FEBRUAR 1933 machte sich der 18 Jahre alte Patrick Leigh Fermor auf, um von Rotterdam nach Konstantinopel zu wandern. Seine Ausrüstung bestand aus einem alten Armee-Überzieher, Pullover, Flanellhemd, Hosen, Gamaschen, dicken Socken und Nagelstiefeln. Zu seinen Luxusgütern gehörten ein Schlafsack, Notizbücher und Bleistifte, ein Wanderstab und der Gedichtband „The Oxford Book of English Verse" – was ihm jedoch alles innerhalb weniger Wochen abhanden kam. Für die ca. 1.500 km lange Reise benötigte er ganze drei Jahre.

Früher oder später hat jeder regelmäßig Reisende einen Gegenstand für sich ausgemacht, der ihn überall hin begleitet – einen Reisebegleiter. Dabei kann es sich um ein spezielles Kissen oder Nackenpolster handeln, ein Schweizer Messer oder ein Fernglas, eine Gürteltasche oder einen Rucksack. Es gibt jene, die ohne Landkarte oder Reiseführer keinen Schritt machen können. Die Bedrohung durch Moskitos oder Hautkrebs zwingt zusätzlich dazu, Insektenspray und Sonnencreme (die moderne Entsprechung des viktorianischen Sonnenschirms) einzupacken. Die Umsichtigen entscheiden sich für ein Erste-Hilfe-Set. Die Abenteurer stellen sicher, dass sie Kompass oder Satellitennavigationssystem dabei haben, da es viele Orte auf der Welt gibt, an denen man sich hoffnungslos verirren kann.

Fermor gab sich mit nichts davon ab. Er nahm ein wenig Geld mit und arrangierte es so, dass er jeden Monat fünf Pfund zur Verfügung hatte, die er an Orten entlang des Weges postlagernd abholen konnte. Wäre er im Stande gewesen, die anfänglichen Aufwendungen aufzubringen, hätte er Reiseschecks benutzen können, die es schon lange gab. Im Jahr 1837 gab Thomas Cook „Umlauf-Noten" heraus, Vorgänger der von *American Express* 1891 ausgegebenen Schecks. Heute ist das Problem der täglichen Finanzierung auf Reisen durch ein 4 x 5 cm großes Stückchen Plastik gelöst. Die Kreditkarte ist vielleicht die größte Reisehilfe aller Zeiten. Mit ihr lassen sich Tickets, Mahlzeiten, Kleidung, Unterkunft, Souvenirs bezahlen und ein scheinbar grenzenloser Vorrat der jeweiligen Landeswährung beschaffen. Das Vergnügen und die Hilfe, die sie bietet, kommt zuerst. Die Rechnung folgt später.

Fermor war einer der seltenen Individualisten, der einsame Reisende. Die Hilfe von Reisebüro oder Reiseleiter war nichts für ihn. Er verschmähte die Dienste des gewaltigen Imperiums, das fast ein Jahrhundert früher durch den Unternehmergeist eines einzelnen Mannes entstand. Am 5. Juli 1841 organisierte Thomas Cook die erste öffentlich beworbene Zugreise. Der Ausflug führte von Leicester zu einer Temperenzler-Versammlung in Loughborough und kostete einen Shilling pro Kopf. Es war ein voller Erfolg. Cook arrangierte weiterhin Trips ans Meer, nach Paris und zu den Schlachtfeldern von Waterloo. 1851 transportierte Cook 165.000 Besucher zur Weltausstellung im Londoner Hyde Park. Bis zum Jahr 1870 veranstaltete er Reisen in nahezu jedes Land der Welt, hatte Verbindungen zu über 500 Hotels und verkaufte Fahrkarten für 344.739 von 369.495 Zugverbindungen weltweit. „Es gibt Flecken auf der Sonne, ABER keinen Fleck auf Erden, den Sie nicht mit Hilfe von Cook's Tickets besuchen können", rühmte eine seiner Anzeigen. Cook war der König des Reisens. „Schutzlose Frauen vertrauen sich ihm an", schrieb ein Zeitgenosse. „Hypochonder erzählen ihm von ihren Leiden, törichte Reisende verlassen sich auf ihn, damit er ihre Fehler wett machen würde..."

Cooks Geschick und Erfolg beim Organisieren von Reisen für die Massen forderte eine Reihe von Konkurrenten heraus. Carl Stangen aus Berlin organisierte 1878 seine erste Weltreise. Sie zog nur sieben Kunden an, doch Stangen hielt durch. Bis 1889 hatte er zahlreiche Teilnehmer für ähnliche Reisen gewonnen, die acht Monate dauerten und mehr als 11.000 Mark kosteten. 1893 organisierte Sir Henry Lunn, Gründer der noch heute unter seinem Namen bestehenden Reiseagentur, seine erste Reise: Sie führte in die Schweiz, denn Lunn war selbst ein begeisterter Bergsteiger. Heute gibt es in jeder Stadt der Welt ein Reisebüro.

Reisende waren zunehmend besser geschützt und besser informiert. Ein völlig neuer Industriezweig entstand, um deren Bedürfnisse zu stillen. Fortnums in London verkaufte 100 kg Kakaopulver an Sir Edward Parry, der 1819 aufbrach, um die Nordwest-Passage zu suchen. In den frühen Dreißiger Jahren des 19. Jahrhunderts eröffnete William James Adams einen Laden in der Fleet Street, wo er alles verkaufte, was ein

Reisender vielleicht benötigen konnte, von Reiseführern und Pässen bis hin zum Insektenpulver. Eine Generation später gründete eine Gruppe von Army- und Navy-Offizieren eine Kooperative, die Militärangehörige und ihre Familien versorgte, mit besonderem Augenmerk auf den Reisebedarf. Man sagte, wer eine Reise antreten wolle, könne in den neuen *Army and Navy Stores* schlicht alles bekommen, von der Nadel bis zum Elefanten.

Einer der ersten Reiseführer war der Frankreich-Reiseführer von Thomas Martyn aus dem Jahr 1787, komplett mit einer Skala von bis zu vier Ausrufezeichen (ähnlich wie die Michelin-Rosetten) zur Bewertung einzelner Gemälde in Galerien und Museen. Die erste professionelle Reiseführer-Autorin hieß Mariana Stokes. Sie veröffentlichte 1820 ihre „Briefe aus Italien". Die berühmteste Reiseführer-Serie war jedoch jene von Carl Baedeker. 1829 erwarb Baedeker einen erfolglosen Verlag, der unter anderem einen „Reiseführer Koblenz" herausgebracht hatte. Ausgehend von diesem bescheidenen Beginn produzierte er Reiseführer für ganz Europa mit dem Ziel, genügend gedruckte Informationen zu liefern, die Reisende in die Lage versetzten, auf die Dienste bezahlter Führer verzichten zu können. Die heutigen *Michelin*, *Rough Guides*, *Fodor's Guides* und *Lonely-Planet-Guides* treten in Baedekers gedruckte Fußstapfen.

Im Kielwasser der Reiseführer folgten Fahrpläne und Landkarten. Die Landkarten des Britischen Landesvermessungsamtes in großem Maßstab erschienen erstmals 1805. Ihr ursprüngliches Ziel war es, die Planung der Verteidigung der englischen Küstenlinie gegen die Invasion Napoleon Bonapartes zu unterstützen, doch schon bald waren sie auch bei Reisenden und Urlaubern beliebt. Die Gebrüder Michelin – immer darauf aus, die Nutzung des Automobils zu propagieren und den Verkauf ihrer Reifen zu steigern – veröffentlichten Landkarten für nahezu ganz Europa. Rand McNally tat dasselbe für Kanada, die Vereinigten Staaten und Mexiko.

CLOCKWISE FROM OPPOSITE
Passengers await their luggage after docking in Fishguard harbour, Wales on the Cunard liner *Mauretania*, August 1909; A selection from travel items from catalogue illustrations: wardrobe trunk from the *Army and Navy Stores* (late 19th century); *Mappin and Webb's* travelling bags with 'silver and ivory fittings' (1886); travelling bags 'of every description' from *Parkins and Gotto* of Oxford Street; An elaborate tea basket from the *Army and Navy Stores* (1932).

AUF DER LINKEN SEITE BEGINNEND IM UHRZEIGERSINN
Passagiere warten nach dem Anlegen des Cunard-Liners *Mauretania* in Fishguard Harbour, Wales, auf ihr Gepäck (August 1909); Eine Auswahl von Reiseartikeln aus verschiedenen Katalogen: Schrankkoffer der *Army and Navy Stores* (Ende des 19. Jahrhunderts); Reisetaschen von *Mappin and Webb's* mit „Silber- und Eisenbeschlägen" (1886); Reisetaschen „aller Art" von *Parkins and Gotto*, Oxford Street; ein kunstvoller Picknickkorb aus den *Army and Navy Stores* (1932).

DANS LE SENS DES AIGUILLES D'UNE MONTRE, A PARTIR DE LA PHOTO CI-CONTRE
Des passagers attendent leur bagage après être arrivés à quai au port Fishguard, Pays de Galles à bord du paquebot *Mauretania* de la compagnie Cunard, août 1909. Sélection d'articles de voyages à partir des illustrations d'un catalogue: coffre à vêtements des magasins *Army and Navy Stores* (fin du 19ème siècle). Sacs de voyage de *Mappin and Webb* avec accessoires en argent et en ivoire (1886). Sacs de voyage en tout genre de *Parkins and Gotto* de Oxford Street. Un panier à thé élaboré provenant des magasins *Army and Navy Stores* (1932).

Four-colour blocks by DIRECT PHOTO-ENGRAVING CO. LTD.   Inks by SHACKELL, EDWARDS & CO. LTD

TEA BASKET
By kind permission of the Army and Navy Co-operative Society.

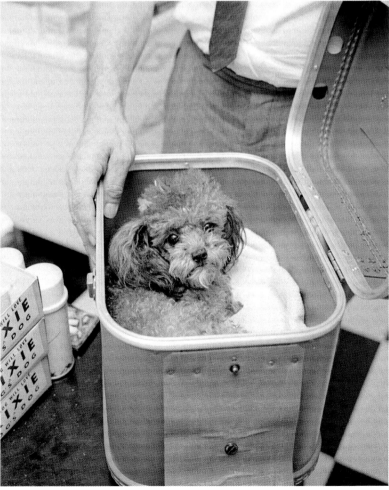

CLOCKWISE FROM BOTTOM LEFT

A grim faced poodle models a doggie carrying case in the lobby of the *New Yorker Hotel*, New York City, USA in September 1964; First on the beach – a dachshund shares a sun-bed with its bronzed owner on a Mediterranean beach, 27th July 1981; The Vuitton dog carrier; Gloria Schiff and friend at Lyford Cay in the Bahamas, 1963.

IM UHRZEIGERSINN VON LINKS UNTEN

Ein grimmiger Pudel ist Model für einen Hundetransportkorb in der Lobby des *New Yorker Hotel*, New York City, USA (September 1964); Die Ersten am Strand – Ein Dackel teilt sich mit seiner gebräunten Besitzerin eine Sonnenliege an einem Mittelmeerstrand (27. Juli 1981); Die Hundetransporttasche von Vuitton; Gloria Schiff mit Freund in Lyford Cay auf den Bahamas (1963).

DANS LE SENS DES AIGUILLES D'UNE MONTRE, A PARTIR DU BAS A GAUCHE

Un caniche à la face rébarbative présente une valise pour chien dans le hall du *New Yorker Hotel*, New York City, USA en septembre 1964. Les premiers sur la plage – un teckel partage le lit-pliant avec sa maîtresse bronzée sur une plage de la Méditerranée, 27 juillet 1981. Sac pour transporter les chiens de Vuitton. Gloria Schiff et son ami à Lyford Cay dans les Bahamas, 1963.

Als Jules Verne 1873 „In Achtzig Tagen um die Welt" schrieb, benutzte er *Bradshaws Rail Guide*, um die kürzeste Zeit auszurechnen, in der eine Umrundung des Globus möglich schien. George Bradshaw stellte Druckstöcke her, war gleichzeitig Drucker und gab 1839 den ersten Zugfahrplan unter seinem Namen heraus. 1847 folgte der erste kontinentale Zug-Reiseführer – sechsundzwanzig Jahre vor Cooks erstem Fahrplan für den Kontinent. Es war eine ungeheure Aufgabe, da die Zuglinien beinahe jeden Monat ihre Fahrpläne änderten und dies ohne große Ankündigung. Doch Bradshaw und seine Mitarbeiter blieben bei der Arbeit und spielten eine große Rolle bei der Aufgabe, Ordnung in das europäische Eisenbahnnetz zu bringen.

Langsam, doch unaufhaltsam entwickelten sich Lösungen für jedes Reiseproblem. Der Jumbojet reduzierte die Kosten für die Reisen von Kontinent zu Kontinent dramatisch. Es kamen Mittel und Medikamente auf den Markt, mit denen die tödlichen Krankheiten der Welt bekämpft werden konnten. Moskitonetze machten den Qualen so mancher tropischen Nacht ein Ende. Ingenieure und Chemiker arbeiteten mit vereinten Kräften daran, Schiffsreisen komfortabler zu machen – erstere durch die Entwicklung von Stabilisatoren, letztere durch Mittel gegen Seekrankheit. 1920 kam *Mothersill's Seasick Remedy* auf den Markt, dem später das *Kwells* genannte Medikament folgte. Doch der wahre Durchbruch erfolgte mit der Einführung eines synthetischen Anti-Histamins namens Dramamine in den vierziger Jahren. Neue Stoffe und Legierungen boten den Rucksacktouristen Zelte, die weniger als ein Kilo wogen. Die Gepäckstücke für weniger rauhe Naturen wurden leichter, dafür aber stabiler. Moderne Kommunikationssysteme machten es möglich, von einer Seite des Globus zur anderen in Kontakt zu bleiben oder um Hilfe zu rufen.

Heute ist die Wirtschaft vieler Länder auf den Tourismus angewiesen. Ganze Land- und Küstengebiete wurden den Bedürfnissen der Reisenden gewidmet. Es gibt jene, die den Overkill fürchten – zu viele reisen zu weit und zu oft. Doch das Schöne und der Reiz daran, sich davon zu machen, bleiben bestehen.

SUNPRUF CREAM
For a gradual pretty tan
without redness. 7/6

Elizabeth Arden

ARDENA POWDER
Summer Shades - Rosetta
Bronze. Light Summer
Sun. 12/6. 20/9.

Eight Hour Cream to soothe and cool the skin after unwise exposure, 6/9

15   PRICE LIST.

**LARGE HAMPER FOR AMBULANCE
STATION AND RAILWAY PURPOSES.**

For contents see next page.

PRICE LIST.   16

THE HAMPER CONTAINS

1 Set of Cane Splints.	1 pair Scissors.
1 Elastic Band Tourniquet.	1 Knife.
½ lb. Carbolic Cotton Wool ... } In Tin Cases.	12 Surgeon's Needles.
½ lb. Boric Lint ... }	1 packet each Safety and Plain Pins.
1 Roll Adhesive Plaster.	½ oz. Carbolised Chinese Twist.
20 Roller Bandages, assorted.	½ oz. Silkworm Gut.
1 doz. Triangular Bandages.	1 reel each Black and White Sewing Thread.
3 Pieces Tape.	
4 oz. Sal Volatile.	1 Kidney-shaped Basin.
4 oz. Bicarbonate of Soda.	1 Stopper Loosener.
4 oz. of Olive Oil.	1 Graduated Measure.
4 oz. Spirit Ether Comp.	1 cake 20 per cent Carbolic Soap.
¼ lb. Tin Powdered Boric Acid.	1 Nail Brush.
4 oz. Tincture Eucalyptus B.P.C.	3 Empty 8 oz. Bottles.
1 pair Pean's Forceps.	

Price complete, £4

CLOCKWISE FROM BOTTOM LEFT
The LARGE HAMPER FOR AMBULANCE STATION AND RAIL-
WAY PURPOSES – a First Aid kit of 1908; The sensual delights
of having sun cream applied, 1975; On guard against the sun,
using Elizabeth Arden products – a poster from 1948;
'Sunshine without insects', thanks to *Fly-Tox*, 1929.

IM UHRZEIGERSINN VON LINKS UNTEN
DER GROSSE ERSTE HILFE-KOFFER FÜR BAHNHOFS- UND
EISENBAHNZWECKE – ein Erste Hilfe-Set von 1908; Die
sinnlichen Freuden von Sonnencreme (1975); Geschützt vor
der Sonne mit Produkten von Elizabeth Arden – ein Plakat
von 1948; „Sonne ohne Insekten" Dank *Fly-Tox* (1929).

DANS LE SENS DES AIGUILLES D'UNE MONTRE, A PARTIR
DU BAS A GAUCHE
LA GRANDE VALISE DE SECOURS POUR LES STATIONS D'AM-
BULANCE ET POUR LES CHEMINS DE FER – une trousse de
secours de 1908. Le plaisir sensuel d'être enduit de crème
solaire, 1975. Paré pour le soleil, avec les produits d'Elizabeth
Arden. « Du soleil sans insectes » grâce à *Fly-tox*, 1929.

134

Du Soleil sans Insectes …

FLY-TOX

TUE TOUS LES INSECTES

EN FÉVRIER 1933, Patrick Leigh Fermor, âgé de 18 ans, entreprit de marcher de Rotterdam à Constantinople. Il avait pour tout bagage un vieux manteau de l'armée, un pull, une chemise de flanelle, des pantalons, des bandes pour les mollets, des grosses chaussettes et des bottines. Ses objets de valeur étaient un sac de couchage, des carnets et des crayons, une canne de marche et *The Oxford Book of English Verse* – Il perdit le tout en quelques semaines. Il lui fallut trois ans pour faire ce voyage de près de mille cinq cents kilomètres.

Tôt ou tard, les voyageurs chevronnés choisissent un objet qu'ils doivent absolument prendre où qu'ils aillent – un compagnon de voyage. Cela peut être un oreiller ou un coussin particulier, un canif suisse ou une paire de jumelles, un sac banane ou un sac à dos. Il y a ceux qui ne supportent pas de faire un pas sans un guide ou une carte. La menace des moustiques ou des mélanomes obligent d'autres à prendre du produit anti-moustiques ou de la crème solaire (l'équivalent moderne du parasol victorien). Les plus prudents prennent une trousse de secours. Les plus aventuriers s'assurent qu'ils ont emporté une boussole ou un système de navigation globale car il existe de nombreux endroits sur terre où l'on peut désespérément se perdre.

Fermor ne s'inquiétait pas de tout cela. Il emmena un peu d'argent et s'arrangea pour trouver chaque mois cinq livres sterling à des adresses poste restante réparties le long de son trajet. Si il avait pu se permettre de payer les frais initiaux, il aurait pu utiliser des chèques de voyage car ils existaient depuis longtemps. En 1873, Thomas Cook mit en circulation des « billets circulaires », qui ont précédé les chèques lancés par American Express en 1891. Aujourd'hui, le problème du financement au jour le jour au cours d'un voyage a été résolu par juste quarante centimètres carrés de plastique. La carte de crédit est peut-être la plus grande assistance de voyage de tous les temps, exerçant sa magie pour obtenir des tickets, des repas, des vêtements, des refuges, des souvenirs et une réserve apparemment illusoire de devises locales. Le plaisir et la commodité qu'elle procure, viennent en premier lieu. La facture suit.

Fermor était un individu rare, un voyageur solitaire. Il n'avait pas besoin de l'assistance d'un agent ou d'un représentant de commerce. Il rejetait avec mépris les services du vaste empire créé près d'un siècle plus tôt par l'entreprise d'un seul homme. Le 5 juillet 1841, Thomas Cook organisait la première excursion en train publiquement commercialisée. L'excursion partait de Leicester vers un rassemblement anti-alcoolique à Loughborough. Le billet coûtait un shilling par personne. Ce fut un succès immédiat. Cook continua à organiser des excursions pour aller à la mer, à Paris, aux champs de bataille de Waterloo. En 1851, Cook transporta 165.000 visiteurs à la grande exposition de Londres à Hyde Park. En 1870, il organisait des voyages dans presque tous les pays du monde, avait des liens commerciaux avec plus de 500 hôtels et vendit des billets à 344.739 compagnies ferroviaires sur les 369.495 compagnies opérant dans le monde. « Il y a des taches solaires, MAIS aucune place sur la terre qu'on ne puisse atteindre avec un billet de Cook » vantait une des publicités de la société. Cook était le roi des voyages. Un contemporain écrivait : « Les femmes sans protection lui font confiance. Les hypocondriaques lui formulent leurs griefs, les voyageurs fous comptent sur lui pour réparer leurs erreurs. »

Le succès et le talent de Cook pour organiser des voyages pour les masses provoqua l'arrivée de concurrents sur le marché. Carl Stangen de Berlin organisait ses premiers tours du monde en 1878. Il n'attira au départ que sept clients, mais Stangen persévéra. En 1889, de nombreux intéressés participaient à de tels tours qui prenaient huit mois et qui coûtaient plus de 11.000 marks. En 1893, Sir Henry Lunn, fondateur de l'agence de voyage qui porte encore son nom, organisait sa première excursion, un voyage en Suisse, car Lunn lui-même était un passionné de montagne. Aujourd'hui il existe une agence de voyage dans chaque ville du monde.

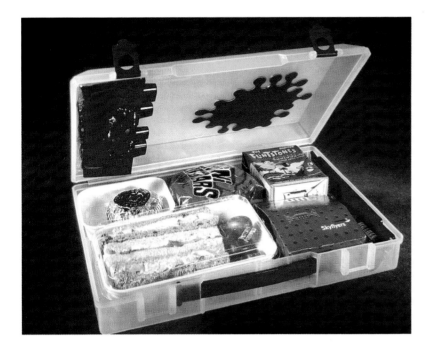

Les voyageurs étaient mieux protégés et mieux informés. Une toute nouvelle industrie vit le jour pour satisfaire à leurs besoins. Fortnums de Londres vendit 100 kilos de poudre de cacao à Sir Edward Parry lorsqu'il entreprit en 1819 la recherche du passage vers le Nord-Ouest. Au début des années trente, Williams James Adams ouvrit un magasin à Fleet Street où il vendait tout ce dont un voyageur pouvait avoir besoin, du guide touristique aux passeports en passant par la poudre contre les insectes. Une génération plus tard, un groupe d'officiers de la marine et de l'armée créait une coopérative qui offrait aux militaires et à leur familles toute sorte d'articles de voyage. On racontait que celui qui avait l'intention de voyager pouvait acheter aussi bien une aiguille qu'un éléphant dans ces nouveaux magasins *Army and Navy Stores*.

Un des premiers guides touristiques était le *Guide de France* de Thomas Martyn en 1787, commenté par une échelle de un à quatre points d'exclamation (comparable aux étoiles du guide Michelin) pour marquer l'importance de tableaux dans les galeries d'art et les musées. Le premier rédacteur professionnel de guides touristiques s'appelait Mariana Stokes, qui publia ses *Lettres d'Italie* en 1820. Toutefois la collection la plus fameuse de guide est celle de Carl Baedeker. En 1829, Baedeker acheta une maison d'édition en faillite, dont l'inventaire comprenait un *Guide de Coblence*. Il continua, après ces modestes débuts, à produire des guides qui couvraient l'ensemble de l'Europe et dont le but était de fournir aux voyageurs assez d'informations imprimées pour qu'ils puissent se passer des services d'un guide payé. Aujourd'hui, les guides *Michelin*, *Rough*, *Fodor's* et les guides de la *Lonely Planet* suivent la voie imprimée de Baedeker.

Après les guides, vinrent les horaires et les cartes. Les cartes à grande échelle de la *British Ordnance Survey* apparurent pour la première fois en 1805. Leur but initial était d'aider à planifier la défense des côtes anglaises contre l'invasion de Napoléon Bonaparte, mais elles devinrent très vite populaires parmi les voyageurs et les vacanciers. Les frères Michelin – toujours enclins à promouvoir l'utilisation de la voiture et par conséquence la vente de leurs pneus – publièrent des cartes de toute l'Europe et Rand McNally fit de même pour le Canada, les États-Unis et le Mexique.

En 1873, lorsque Jules Verne écrivait la trame de *Le Tour du monde en quatre-vingts jours*, il utilisa le Guide ferroviaire de Bradshaw afin de calculer le temps nécessaire minimum pour faire le tour du globe. George Bradshaw était un graveur et imprimeur qui publia les premiers Horaires des Chemins de Fer à porter son

FRÜHSTÜCK	BREAKFAST
Grape Fruit Apfelsinen	Grape Fruit Oranges
Weintrauben	Grapes
Tomatensaft Gedünst. Pflaumen	Tomato Juice Stewed Prunes
Haferflocken Haferschleim	Porridge Oatmeal Gruel
Hominy in Milch	Hominy in Milk
Shredded Wheat Corn Flakes	Shredded Wheat Corn Flakes
Rice Krispies	Rice Krispies
Buchweizen-Griddle-Keks	Buckwheat Griddle Cakes
mit Ahorn-Sirup	with Maple Syrup
Deutscher Pfannkuchen	German Pancake
Kreolen-Pfannkuchen	Pancake Créole
Setzeier auf beiden Seiten gebrat.	Shirred Eggs Turned Over
Rührei Lesseps oder einfach	Scrambled Eggs Lesseps or Plain
Omelette mit feinen Kräutern	Omelette with Fine Herbs
Gebackene Eier amerikanisch	Fried Eggs American Style
Gekochte Eier	Boiled Eggs
Poschierte Salzmakrele Whitemore	Poach. Salted Mackerel Whitemore
Schweinsfilet, Sauce Robert,	Tenderloin of Pork, Sauce Robert,
Haschee-Kartoffeln	Hashed Potatoes
Vom Rost (etwa 5 bis 6 Minuten)	From the Grill (about 5 to 6 Min.)
Yorker Schinken	Yorkshire Ham
Black Hawk Speck	Black Hawk Bacon
Kalte Speisen	Cold Dishes
Wiener Braten, Rote Beete	Vienna Minced Roast, Beetroot
Thüringer Preßkopf in Essig u. Oel	Thuringian Pig's Head Vinaigrette
Verschiedene Wurst	Choice of Sausage
Gournay-Käse	Gournay Cheese
Dreifrucht- u. Orangen-Marmelade	Three Fruit Jam Orange Marmalade
Brombeergelee	Bramble-berry Jelly
Aprikosen-Konfitüre Honig	Apricot Confiture Honey
Frühstücks-Gebäck Röstbrot	Breakfast Pastry Toast
Graham-Brot	Graham Bread
Schnecken Hörnchen	Schnecken Crescents
Kaffee Milch Maté Tee	Coffee Milk Maté Tea
Englisch.Frühstücks- u.Ceylon-Tee	English Breakfast and Ceylon Tea
Malzkakao	Malted Cocoa

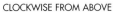

CLOCKWISE FROM ABOVE

A waiter summons passengers to the dining car on the
Canadian Pacific Railroad, 24th June 1939; The breakfast menu
from the original *Norddeutscher-Lloyd Line Bremen*; A set of
coupons issued by *Thos Cook and Co* to cover the cost of
meals and accommodation in one of their accredited hotels,
back in the 19th century; Poster and pudding from the Venice-
Simplon *Orient Express*; Wedgewood china for First Class passengers on *British Airways*, September 2000; A children's
lunchbox from *British Airways*; A 'cover' for one on board a
luxury train, with *Wagon-lits* menu, and china from the *Fleche
d'Or* and *Le Train Bleu*.

OBEN BEGINNEND IM UHRZEIGERSINN

Ein Kellner bittet Passagiere in den Speisewagen der *Canadian
Pacific Railroad* (24. Juni 1939); Die Frühstückskarte der
Bremen der Reederei *Norddeutscher Lloyd*; Coupons von *Thos
Cook and Co.* für Mahlzeiten und Unterbringung in einem
ihrer angeschlossenen Hotels (19. Jahrhundert); Plakat und
Pudding vom Venedig-Simplon *Orient Express*; Wegdewood-
Porzellan für die Erste-Klasse-Passagiere der *British Airways*
(September 2000); Lunchbox für Kinder von *British Airways*;
Gedeck für Reisende eines Luxuszuges mit Speisekarte von
Wagon-lits und Porzellan von *Fleche d'Or* und *Le Train Bleu*.

DANS LE SENS DES AIGUILLES D'UNE MONTRE, À PARTIR
DU HAUT

Un serveur prie les passagers de se rendre dans le wagon-
restaurant de la *Canadian Pacific Railroad*, 24 juin 1939.
Menu du petit déjeuner des premières croisières du
Norddeutscher Lloyd, Bremen. Retour au 19ème siècle, une
série de chèques délivrés par *Thos Cook and Co* pour couvrir
les frais de restauration et de logement dans un de ses
hôtels accrédités. Poster et pudding de l' *Orient Express*
Venise-Simplon. De la porcelaine de *Wedgewood* pour les
passagers de la première classe de la *British Airways*, septembre 2000. Une boîte-repas pour les enfants de la *British
Airways*. Une couvert à bord d'un train de luxe, avec le menu
des *Wagons-lits* et de la porcelaine de la *Flèche d'Or* et du
Train Bleu.

nom en 1839 et son premier Guide Ferroviaire Continental en 1847 – vingt-six ans avant que ne paraissent les premiers Horaires Continentaux de Cook. Il s'agissait d'une tâche monumentale puisque les compagnies de chemins de fer modifiaient leurs horaires presque chaque mois avec peu d'avertissement préalable, mais Bradshaw et ses assistants s'attelèrent à la tâche et contribuèrent ainsi à remettre de l'ordre dans le réseau ferroviaire européen.

Lentement mais sûrement, des solutions étaient apportées à tous les problèmes liés aux voyages. Le coût des voyages intercontinentaux furent considérablement réduits grâce aux jumbo jet. Les médicaments furent accessibles pour combattre les maladies mortelles du monde entier. Les moustiquaires apaisèrent les tourments de nombreuses personnes pendant les nuits tropicales. Les ingénieurs et les chimistes unirent leurs forces pour rendre les voyages en mer plus confortables – les premiers en développant des stabilisateurs pour les bateaux, les derniers en créant des remèdes contre le mal de mer. Le remède contre le mal de mer de Mothersill apparut pour la première fois en 1920, suivi ensuite par les remèdes appelés *Kwells*, mais la réelle percée eut lieu avec l'invention en 1940 d'un antihistaminique de synthèse appelé dramamine. De nouveaux tissus et alliages allégèrent le sac à dos des voyageurs avec des tentes pesant moins d'un kilo. Les bagages devinrent en général plus légers tout en étant plus robustes. Les moyens de communication modernes permirent de garder le contact et d'appeler à l'aide dans tous les coins du monde.

À l'heure actuelle, l'économie de nombreux pays repose sur le tourisme et de nombreuses régions, à la campagne ou à la côte, ont été spécialement aménagées pour les besoins du touriste. Certains craignent l'exagération – certains poussent les limites trop souvent trop loin. Toutefois, chaque décollage reste synonyme de splendeur et de fascination.

CLOCKWISE FROM ABOVE RIGHT
Neatly labelled toppers and bowlers get a ride in the service lift at London's *Savoy Hotel*, 1925; An attendant at the Lost Property Office on Waterloo Station, London displays a small selection of the debris that travellers leave behind; Thirteen lucky finalists in the *Miss New York Aviation Contest* visit the UN building, 1965; A flight attendant of the 1960s practises serving coffee – it's tougher at 30,000 feet.

IM UHRZEIGERSINN VON RECHTS OBEN
Ordentlich beschriftete Zylinder und Melonen im Service-Aufzug des Londoner *Savoy Hotels* (1925); Ein Mitarbeiter des Fundbüros im Bahnhof von Waterloo zeigt eine kleine Auswahl der Dinge, die Reisende so liegen lassen; Dreizehn glückliche Finalistinnen des *Miss New York Aviation Contest* besuchen das UN-Gebäude (1965); Eine Flugbegleiterin in den Sechziger Jahren übt das Servieren von Kaffee – gar nicht so einfach in 30.000 Fuß Höhe.

DANS LE SENS DES AIGUILLES D'UNE MONTRE, A PARTIR DU HAUT A DROITE
Des haut-de-forme et des chapeaux melon soigneusement éti-quetés empruntent l'ascenseur de service au *Savoy Hotel* de Londres, 1925. Un employé du bureau des objets trouvés de la gare de Waterloo à Londres montre une petite sélection des objects que les voyageurs peuvent laisser traîner. Les treize heureuses finalistes du concours de *Miss New York Aviation* visitent les bâtiments des Nations Unies en 1965. Une hôtesse de l'air s'entraîne à servir le café dans les années soixante – c'est beaucoup plus difficile à 30.000 pieds d'altitude.

ACKNOWLEDGEMENTS

Getty Images is the world's leading visual content provider with 70 million images and 30,000 hours of film footage held by the various collections. The archival resources are held by HultonlArchive , who has provided many of the images for this book. With over 40 million images, HultonlArchive is an unparalleled resource of unique illustrative material covering every facet of people's experiences and environment, recording history to the present day.

American Express: Co. 41 bottom
Baedeker GmbH: 123 top middle
Carnival Cruise Lines: 33
Club 18-30: 65 top
Thomas Cook Archives: 137 bottom right
Mary Evans Picture Library: 35 top right, 76 bottom right, 79 top left, 117 bottom, 121 left, 123 bottom left, middle left, 124 all, 125 top right, middle left, 128 hotel labels, 131 top right, bottom right, bottom left, 134 top right, bottom, 135
Getty Images: Slim Aarons Front cover, 3, 4, 16 bottom, 29, 36, 37, 46-7, 59, 66-8, 82-3, 102, 104, 111, 112 left, 113 bottom, 115, 118-19, 133 right, 141; Alan Band 98; Ruth Cushman 34; Alexander Czechatz/Heinrich Bauer Verlag 110; William England 56-7; Tamás Fényes 71; Ernst Haas 6, 54, 80, 94-5, 106; Vagin Hansen 74; Slim Hewitt 144; Hirz 18; Peter Keegan 127 top right; Victor Keppler/George Eastman House 121 left; Lambert 122 bottom, 134 top left; Dorothea Lange 7; Felix Man 109; Douglas Miller Back cover; PA Interpress Photos 126; John Reardon/The Observer 79 right; Dick Smith 108; Svenskt Pressfoto 107; Scot Swanson Collection 50; Marion Post Walcott 101 top left and Volkmar Wentzel 129
GUAS HF 6/9: 131 top left
NewsCast: 136 top left, middle left
Orient-Express Trains & Cruises: 30 top, 136 bottom left
P&O Steam Navigation Company: 35 top left, 97 top right, 125 bottom left
Panos: Trygve Bølstad 89, Chris Stowers 63, 81, Dermot Tatlow 78
Rough Guide Ltd.: 123 top right
Stone: Dale Boyer 101 bottom right; John Callahan 85; Nicholas DeVore 69; Graeme Harris 93; Yann Layma 97 top left; Mark Lewis 39; Charles Mason 20 middle; Josh Mitchell 96; Vito Palmisano 101 bottom left; Bert Sagara 23; Chris Sanders 75; Stephen Swintek 138 top right; Baron Wolman 97 bottom and Ted Wood 100 right
Louis Vuitton: 133 left
All other images © Getty Images

Special thanks for their assistance to Liz Ihre, James Charnock and Elin Hagström

OVERLEAF

Heading for home – a young holidaymaker recovers on a train after the fun and exhaustion of a day at the seaside as summer draws to its close, 14th September 1946.

ABOVE

Slim Aarons sets out on a two-wheeled photographic quest during the filming of *Mr Roberts* in Hawaii, 1955.

FOLGENDE SEITE

Auf dem Weg nach Hause – ein junger Urlauber erholt sich am Ende des Sommers im Zug von anstrengenden Ferientagen am Meer (14. September 1946).

OBEN

Slim Aarons macht sich während der Dreharbeiten zu „Mr. Roberts" auf zwei Rädern auf Motivsuche in Hawaii (1955).

AU VERSO

De retour à la maison – un jeune vacancier se remet de la fatigue d'une journée d'amusement au bord de la mer alors que l'été touche à sa fin, 14 septembre 1946.

EN HAUT

Slim Aarons se met en route pour une quête photographique sur deux roues pendant le tournage de « Mr Roberts » à Hawaii en 1955.

INDEX